Carleton Renaissance Plays in Translation

General Editors: Donald Beecher, Massimo Ciavolella

Editorial Advisors: Douglas Campbell (Carleton), Peter Clive (Carleton), Louise George Clubb (Berkeley), Bruno Damiani (Catholic University of America), Louise Fothergill-Payne (Calgary), Peter Fothergill-Payne (Calgary), Amilcare Iannucci (Toronto), Jean-Marie Maguin (Montpellier), Domenico Pietropaolo (Toronto), Anthony Raspa (Chicoutimi), Leonard Sbrocchi (Ottawa), Pamela Stewart (McGill).

Carleton Renaissance Plays in Translation offer the student, scholar, and general reader a selection of sixteenth-century masterpieces in modern English translations, most of them for the first time. The texts have been chosen for their intrinsic merits and for their importance in the history of the development of the theatre. Each volume contains a critical and interpretative introduction intended to increase the enjoyment and understanding of the text. Reading notes illuminate particular references, allusions, and topical details.

In print:

Carleton Renaissance Plays in Translation

Lope de Vega

THE DUCHESS OF AMALFI'S STEWARD
(El mayordomo de la duquesa de Amalfi)

Translated, with an Introduction and Notes, by
Cynthia Rodriguez-Badendyck

Published for the Carleton University Centre for
Renaissance Studies and Research by

Dovehouse Editions Canada
1985

Canadian Cataloguing in Publication Data

Vega, Lope de, 1562-1635
  The duchess of Amalfi's steward

(Carleton Renaissance plays in translation ; 8)
Translation of: El mayordomo de la duquesa de Amalfi.
Bibliography: p. 41
ISBN 0-919473-53-9

I. Title. II. Series.

PQ6439.M35 1985   862'.3   C86-090053-3

For information on distribution and for all orders write to:
      Dovehouse Editions, Canada
      32 Glen Ave.
      Ottawa, Canada
      K1S 2Z7

For further information about the series write to:
      The Editors, Carleton Renaissance Plays in Translation
      Carleton Centre for Renaissance Studies
      1812 Arts Tower
      Carleton University
      Ottawa, Canada
      K1S 5B6

Acknowledgements

This text owes its earliest and greatest debt to the late Professor Hannah Bergman of the City University of New York Graduate Center, who first suggested that I translate Golden Age plays and introduced me to this one. Without her help, support, and warm encouragement, I should never have made it through the journeyman stages. I owe an enormous debt, likewise, to Professor Alan Trueblood of Brown University, who was kind enough to be remorseless with my translation. He has saved me from many a blunder and provided invaluable illuminations and suggestions from his long familiarity with Lope. Thanks must be given also to Professor Gregory Rabassa. It was he who convinced me that translation could be (among other things) a lark. The courtesy and professionalism of Professors Donald Beecher and Massimo Ciavolella of the Carleton Renaissance Centre have eased the inevitable agonies in the preparation of the manuscript. Their infectious enthusiasm for the field of Renaissance theatre is itself a resource.

To Professors Alicia Ramos, James Crapotta, and Laura Hapke and to Mr. Edward Plunkett goes my deep appreciation for their comments on the text and on the introduction. To my friend and colleague Barbara Shollar, thanks which only she can understand for her careful and professional proofreading of the whole.

The opportunity provided by New York's Tudor City Players, who allowed me to direct their staged reading of the play, gave me new insights into the play as performance and the text as spoken language. I do not know how to thank my son, Thor, for consenting to play Alejandro despite his misgivings (however, I'm sure he will think of something). His very young noble manliness and the frail solemnity of Rachel Braun as his sister brought tears to more eyes than mine, and showed how extraordinarily astute Lope was about using children on a stage.

Finally, a special acknowledgement must go to Professor Lawrence Badendyck, an archive of general information and a miraculous obtainer of books and sources as well as a supportive spouse, without whom, etc.

DEDICATION

INTRODUCTION

Life

Considerable documentation exists about the life of Lope de Vega, who achieved great celebrity in his own time; and although some of the poet's claims about his own life, as well as the claims of his friend and biographer, Juan Pérez de Montalván, are now questioned or even dismissed, enough reliable evidence survives to give scholars a much more vivid and complex portrait of this singular genius as man and artist than we can piece together from the meagre records left us about Calderón or Shakespeare.

Lope Félix de Vega Carpio was born in Madrid on November 25, 1562, two years before Shakespeare. The son of middle-class parents (his father was an embroiderer) originally from the mountainous north of Spain, Lope was educated at the *Colegio de los Teatinos* and later at the University of Alcalá. We are told he was a precocious student of mathematics as well as languages, but most significantly that he was from a very early age a prodigy at writing verses. Before he could actually write, he would pay older students with portions of his breakfast to take down his verses for him. He wrote fluently in Latin as well as Spanish, read Italian and possibly French, and composed his first play, *El verdadero amante* (*The True Lover*) when he was twelve — according to his own account.

Lope's father, Félix de Vega Carpio, appears to have been a man of remarkable charity, who, with his children, would daily visit the *Buen Suceso* hospital in Madrid. There the pious family would make beds, sweep and clean the corridors, wash the feet and hands of the poor, and console the convalescent, dressing them and helping them with gifts.[1] Of Lope's mother, Francisca Fernández Flores, we know little.

When Lope was sixteen, however, his father died, and the young poet entered upon a restless period, lived with a choleric uncle in Seville, got into scrapes with a friend, and began to publish *romances*. The *romance*, or ballad, was an old popular form then

enjoying a vogue among the literati, and Lope's grace and fluency
in the medium, along with a gift for dialogue and dramatic
stiuation, earned him a small reputation. To make ends meet,
Lope entered service with the Bishop of Avila, and for the Bishop's amusement began to scribble plays again. First imitating and
then modifying the work of early sixteenth-century actor/play-
wrights, he began to develop the conventions of the new type of
play or *comedia*, which was to usher in the Golden Age of drama in
Spain.

When Lope was in his early twenties he became the principal
in a scandalous series of events which were to leave a profound
mark on him as an artist.[2] Since we have two remarkable records
of the incidents — one an autobiographical dramatic novel, *La
Dorotea*, begun soon after the events and revised near the end of
his life, and the other a series of transcripts from the lawcase that
climaxed the affair — we are able to follow the story in unusual
detail. It appears that about the middle of the 1580's Lope became
romantically involved with Elena Osorio, a married woman somewhat older than he, the daughter of a well-known Madrid actor/
manager. Contrary to the honour conventions presented on the
stage, neither her father nor her husband appears to have presented any obstacle to the affair for about four years, and Lope celebrated their love extensively in verse — thinly disguising Elena
under the pastoral name of *Filis* and himself under the name
Belardo (a name he continued to use throughout his career for his
own persona in fiction).

Some time in the spring of 1588, however, pressure appears
to have been brought upon Elena to accept the attentions of a
wealthy *indiano*, a Spaniard who had earned his fortune in the
New World. Whether as cause or as effect of this, Lope began selling his plays to other managers. Attempts by the rival lovers to
"share" Elena proved intolerable, and in a rage of jealousy and hu-
miliation the young poet turned loose a series of scurrilous verses
in macaronic Latin against his erstwhile mistress and her family,
branding her a prostitute and her family procurers who lived off
her gains. The family took him to court.

Lope was convicted and sentenced to exile from Madrid for
six years and from Castile for two. In prison his conduct was so in-
corrigible that the exile was extended for another two years. Not
only did this affair cause him to move his residence to Valencia,
but the pattern of the romantic rejection recurs over and over
again in his work. Nor did exile end the episodes of real-life
drama. Within months he had sneaked back into Madrid to abduct

Isabel de Urbina (celebrated in his verse as *Belisa*), the daughter of the king-of-arms to Philip II. Although Isabel was not a duchess, her parents had reason to see her marriage to a publically disgraced embroiderer's son as distinctly declassé. In addition, by breaking the terms of his exile, Lope risked arrest and execution. Isabel was shortly after returned to her parents, and under the circumstances they consented to her marriage on May 10, 1588 by proxy, the bridegroom having escaped arrest (for abduction this time) and returned to Valencia. Although *The Duchess of Amalfi's Steward* is clearly based upon an Italian source, it is not difficult to see in the incidents surrounding this marriage experiences which would increase the artist's sympathy with his story.

Nineteen days after the wedding, the Armada against England left Lisbon harbour. Some scholars question Lope's repeated assertions that he and his brother set sail with that famous expedition, and that his brother was killed in the fighting, but there is no evidence he was elsewhere. Although to have survived would seem feat enough, Lope further claims to have written *La hermosura de Angelica (The Beauty of Angelica)*, his verse-epic sequel to Ariosto, on board the *San Juan*.

The exiled poet spent several crucial years in Valencia with his wife, and his influence on the theatre of that city was considerable, as was its influence on him. But he was eventually pardoned both for the libel and the abduction (and the breaking of exile) and allowed to return to the capital. It is interesting to note that the petition to rescind the libel suit was made by Elena's actor/manager father. Lope's value as a supplier of plays may well have had something to do with this change of heart.

In contrast to a personal life fraught with incident and scandal, Lope's life as an artist was unusually stable. Remarkably early he established himself as the premier playwright of Spain, and he maintained that position — not without challenge, but certainly without rout — until he died in his bed at the age of seventy-three. His great contemporary Quevedo tells us that even during his lifetime the name *Lope* became a colloquial synonym for excellence.[3] Nor was his phenomenal output limited to plays, although plays made his lasting reputation. He tried his hand at virtually every literary form available to the time, with mixed success, but never without skill.

In 1596, his wife having died in childbirth, Lope was indicted for criminal concubinage with one Antonia Trillo in Madrid. But the real love of this period appears to have been an actress named Micaela de Lujan, called in his verses *Lucinda*, who bore him two talented children, Lope Félix and Marcela. In 1598 he married his second wife, Juana de Guardo, the daughter of a wealthy pork butcher.

By 1603 Lope's name was so much in the ascendant that plays by lesser dramatists were often passed off as his or pirated in part by individuals such as the one called *Gran Memoria*, who would memorize passages by sitting in the audience and then invent the rest. A famous actor named Sánchez, we are told, stopped in the middle of a performance of one of Lope's plays, hearing that *Gran Memoria* was in the audience; he refused to proceed until the man was expelled.[4] In such a climate a volume speciously titled *Six Plays by Lope de Vega* was published in 1603. Perhaps one out of the six is actually by our author. In 1604 Part I of the *Comedias of Lope de Vega* was published, although probably without his consent.

While Lope earned a fairly steady income from his play-wrighting, at least as long as the theatres were open, the income never seemed to be sufficient for his needs, in part because he had dependents to support (sometimes children in more than one household), in part because he gave prodigally to charity, in part because he needed to keep up certain appearances in dress and amenities. Therefore it was usually necessary for him to obtain a second income by employing himself as secretary to some noble patron such as the Duke of Alba or the nobleman who later became Count of Lemos and Cervantes' patron. In 1605, however, Lope met the young Duke of Sessa, who was to become his patron and friend for the next thirty years. At twenty-six, the Duke was some seventeen years the poet's junior, but he shared Lope's two abiding passions: poetry and love affairs. Lope performed secretarial services and also wrote the Duke's love letters, a task he continued to perform even after taking holy orders, until, in fact, his confessor convinced him that he risked his immortal soul in doing so. The correspondence of three decades between the two is an intimate and revealing one.

In 1609 Lope delivered an address to the Academy of Madrid called *El arte nuevo de hacer comedias en este tiempo* (*The New Art of Writing Plays in These Times*), a verse manifesto of something under four hundred lines which, although written with some irony, is a valuable document in revealing Lope's conscious attitude towards playwrighting, the classical unities, and "the wrath of the seated Spaniard." He deliberately set aside the second in order to placate the third.

In 1614, after the death of his second wife, Lope took holy orders as a priest.

In 1617, the year after Shakespeare's death, Lope's youngest daughter was born to another man's wife.

About this time Lope had begun to realize the importance of his popular dramatic production, which he had consistently disparaged in favour of his more academic literary works. Part IX of the *Comedias of Lope de Vega*, published in 1617, is the first issued by Lope himself. Two more parts followed in quick succession, our play, *The Duchess of Amalfi's Steward*, first appearing in Part XI in 1618. All told, between 1604 and 1647, twelve years after the poet's death, twenty-five parts were published, containing some dozen plays apiece. Part XX (1630) was the last published by Lope in his lifetime, although he prepared XXI (1635), which was published after his death by his daughter Feliciana. These Parts constitute our primary sources for Lope's *comedias*. The total from these, other printed sources, and some two dozen plays in manuscript, comes to over four hundred. This figure does not include the allegorical religious pieces called *autos*, or the numerous prologues, interludes, and other minor pieces attributed to him.

Lope was from the beginning of his career actively involved in the intellectual life of the country, was impressed into all the short-lived literary societies, presided over poetical "jousts," and knew the major writers of his time, most of whom he praised fulsomely in his *Laurel de Apollo*. Yet he had his rivals and enemies, with whom he often engaged in satiric squabbles in verse. Although he stooped to ridicule Alarcón's physical deformity, he lived in fear of Gongora's disemboweling pen and nervously spoke well of him. With Cervantes he had nasty literary exchanges. He borrowed the great novelist's spectacles at a meeting once and found them "like badly poached eggs."[5] His longtime aspiration was to obtain a post at court, particularly to become the royal historian, but these hopes were never fulfilled, and he had to content himself with writing plays (or in one instance an opera) for court festivities.

By 1619 the husband of his last mistress (the accomplished Marta de Nevares, called in his poems *Amarilis*) had died. But Lope, conscious of his priestly vows, was already struggling to make their love platonic. In 1628 Marta lost her sight, and finally her mind. Now old and chastened, his popularity as a playwright dimmed, although not yet eclipsed, by the movement towards the baroque, Lope continued to care for her and for their daughter, Antonia Clara. In 1632 Marta died, and Lope published his dramatic novel, *La Dorotea*, the transformed story of his youthful affair with Elena Osorio.

In 1634 Lope's son, Lope Félix, was killed in a naval engagement. The same year his beloved daughter, Antonia Clara, ran off
with a young nobleman. The same year he published the *Gato-
maquia* (*Catiad*), an enduringly popular satire on Italian epics, with
a cast of cats. On August 23, 1635, Lope wrote his last sonnets,
watered his garden, whipped himself for the last time, and took to
his bed. Four days later, August 27, he died. His property and the
rights to publication of his plays fell to his only surviving legitimate
daughter, Feliciana. His daughter Marcela, a gifted poet, was a
nun. Her father's elaborate funeral procession, financed by the
Duke of Sessa, was diverted to file past the convent gates.

Achievement and Influence

Lope de Vega was not merely a major artist, but like his country-
man Pablo Picasso, a kind of tidal force, a phenomenon of energy
and productivity whose enormous and powerful personal accom-
plishment thrust the art of his age into a new direction. "Necessity
and I," Lope wrote, "going into the business of making verses,
brought the *comedias* into fashion; I drew them from their mean
beginnings, engendering more poets in Spain than there are atoms
in the sunbeam."[6] He might as readily have said, "writing more
plays than there are atoms in a sunbeam," for he was so prolific as
to stagger credulity. He claimed to have written fifteen hundred
plays, but his approach to numbers was somewhat cavalier, and
there is no way of verifying this figure. Still, we have something
over four hundred of his full-length plays surviving in printed or
manuscript form, and we know we have by no means every play he
wrote. Moreover, in addition to his three-act *comedias*, one-act religious *autos*, prologues and interludes, Lope produced a daunting
body of non-theatrical work: novels, short stories, epics, sonnets,
ballads and burlesques, not to mention thirty years of lively correspondence with and for the Duke of Sessa. "A monster of nature,"
Cervantes called him.

Some might wonder if the almost dropsical avidity of the
Spanish public for theatrical performances at the end of the sixteenth century created by its very need the prodigy that was Lope
de Vega. But whether this is true, or whether it was Lope, ontologi-
cally first, whose inordinate genius it was to stimulate inordinate
appetite, is a chicken-and-egg dispute. What matters in the end is
that Lope's work represents an exceptional symbiosis between the
playwright and his public. Lope did not bully his audience or press

an idiosyncratic vision upon them. Rather he so delighted to write and so desired others to delight in what he did that he courted his public, making their own inclinations his best ally. In this regard one may see his numerous, passionate, and shamelessly publicized love affairs as contiguous with his genius as a dramatic poet: he was simply the greatest seducer of audiences who ever lived.

All of his precepts, as set forth in the *New Art of Writing Plays* and as manifest in his work, have a single object: to get and to keep the willing engagement of an audience. The reduction of the number of acts from four to three, for example, did not in fact constitute a reduction of the play, since early four-acts (Lope tells us) were roughly sixteen folio pages long, which is roughly *The Steward*'s length. Rather it involved a radical re-thinking of a play's structure and pacing. In addition, intervals between the acts — Golden Age theatres being short on the amenities of rest rooms and smoking lobbies — were traditionally filled by relaxing *entremeses* or interludes, usually light, farcical, or "low" in content. A reduction in the number of acts reduced these interruptions and increased the emphasis on the play itself.

Seemingly didactic precepts such as the assignment of specific verse forms to specific situations — *redondillas* for love duets, for example, sonnets for reflection — are not restrictive in intent, but merely tricks that work. In fact the shifting of rhyme and rhythm patterns within the play gives Lope's verse a musical variety of the kind that Shakespeare reaches for in shifting from rhyme to blank verse and from blank verse to prose.

The deliberate practice of withholding the denouement until the last possible moment, in marked contrast to some of Shakespeare's plays (one thinks at once of *Cymbeline*), is initially a device to keep an audience from leaving early. And although we can see, especially in *The Steward*, how such a device goes on to affect powerfully the vision of the play, sustaining an extraordinary quality of hope and open possibilities in Lope's work, the vision is pragmatically grounded in his instinctive recognition of the playwright's quasi-romantic relationship to the capricious playgoer: if she is bored, she will leave you.

The figure of the irrepressible *gracioso* or comic servant, also called the *figura del donaire*, was one of Lope's best-loved contributions to the theatre. Both *gracioso* (gracious, witty) and *donaire* (charm and grace) are terms suggesting elegance, a seemingly unlikely attribute for a "downstairs" character. Yet what Lope did was in fact to refine and sophisticate the comic buffoon, replacing the churl who raises laughter by his clumsiness, with a native wit who sees through foolishness at all levels of society and is unimpressed by either pomp or pompousness. This character so captured the affection of audiences that it became almost indispensable in one form or another, male or female. Golden Age plays which fail to include one are in the minority.

In terms of themes, those which Lope felt to be most effective on the stage were, not surprisingly, honour and love; and these themes were taken up not only by a host of Spanish playwrights, but by other continental playwrights who felt the Spanish influence as well, including Racine, Corneille, and the German Romantics. Lope's concern with the depiction of social conventions and pretensions, likewise, can be traced into the satires of Molière.

But the two elements of Lope's art which most immediately charmed an audience were the radiant naturalness and fluidity of his verse and, after the flat stock characters of the old tradition — the dazzling vitality, immediacy, and humanity of his characters. He created a new model for stage characters that had not only strengths, weaknesses, and motivations, but a myriad of finer shadings: subtle wit, self-awareness, shifts of mood and attention, warmth, ruefulness, responsiveness, and, above all, the quality of being actively involved with one another. Masters who followed him, such as Tirso de Molina, Calderón de la Barca, and Rojas Zorrilla, learned to shade characters after his example.

Furthermore, with his almost superhuman literary output, Lope was inevitably a mine of ideas for other writers. Just as generations of painters turned to the Sistine Chapel, quarrying Michelangelo for figures and attitudes, so generations of playwrights quarried Lope, who was during his lifetime translated into French, Italian, Dutch, and even Nahuatl.

Any discussion of Lope's achievement and influence tends to circle back to the almost mythic dimensions of his written production. His contemporaries called him "The Phoenix of Intellects." Anecdotes of his feats of compositional speed abound. Subsequently, study itself has been daunted by the enormous extent of his canon. Indeed, pioneer *Lopista* James Fitzmaurice Kelly must console even as he exhorts, assuring future generations that reading all of Lope de Vega will be a lifetime well spent.[7] Exhaustive Lope scholarship, in short, will always be a task for the few, the gallant, the strong.

Furthermore, while scholars thus far concur on some twenty or thirty plays (roughly what we have from Shakespeare) as the masterpieces of Lope's vast production, even the titles of these relative few are by and large unfamiliar to English-speaking readers.

Despite Lope's acknowledged status as one of the greatest and most influential playwrights in the history of the stage, only a dozen or so of his plays have appeared in published English translations in this century,[8] and of these only *Fuenteovejuna* — a powerful study of rebellion against injustice, in which the hero is an entire village — and *The Knight of Olmedo* (*El caballero de Olmedo*) — a haunting tragedy based on an old *romance* — are listed in *Books in Print* as of this writing. From library sources some may also be familiar with *Peribañez, Justice without Revenge* (*El castigo sin venganza*), *The Star of Seville* (*La estrella de Sevilla*),[9] *The Stupid Lady* (*La dama boba*), *The King the Greatest Alcalde* (*El mejor alcalde, el rey*), and *Madrid Steel* (*El acero de Madrid*). *The Dog in the Manger* (*El perro del hortelano*), a witty "cape and sword" play, is especially interesting in regard to *The Steward*, since it tells the story of a noblewoman who falls in love with her secretary, foists him upon an old lord as a long-lost "son," and marries him without loss of honour.

In contrast to the intimidating size of the canon, with its immense variety and inventiveness, individual works such as *The Steward* are neither titanic, nor overpowering, nor bewildering. On the contrary, they are extraordinarily accessible, intimate, and human in concerns and in scale. This is the paradox of Lope's eminently theatrical achievement, his ability to celebrate, over and over again, this person, this emotion, this moment.

Sources

The primary source for *The Steward* was a narrative, in essence true, made available in Italian in 1554 as story number twenty-six in the first part of the *Novelle* of Matteo Bandello under the descriptive title, "Il signor Antonio Bologna sposa la duchesa d'Amalfi, e tutti due sono ammazzati." Bandello may also have known either the original Antonio or a friend of the original Antonio's from whom he obtained the details of the steward's life. In addition, Bandello himself, disguised in his own story as a gentleman named Delio, probably witnessed the steward's murder on the street near the church of St. Francis in Milan. Bandello speaks highly of Antonio's character and accomplishments, notably as a musician, horseman, and soldier, and indicates further that the steward was a big man, well-built and extremely handsome. Lope would most likely have read Bandello in the original Italian.

Other ideas, notably the display of severed heads in the last act, were probably taken by Lope from Giovanni Battista Giraldi

Cinthio's tragedy of Oronte and Orbecche. Lope would have been familiar with the novella version in Cinthio's *Ecatommiti*.

Text

The Duchess of Amalfi's Steward was written between 1599 and 1606, probably after 1604.[10] It was published under Lope's own supervision in 1618 as one of a dozen plays contained in Part XI of his *Comedias*. The present translation has made use of the Real Academia Española's edition, volume XV of the *Obras de Lope de Vega*.

Golden Age Theatres and Audiences

The Spanish theatre of the Golden Age has roots in popular and secular, as well as classical, traditions, but it owes its establishment as an institution to the pageantry of Medieval Christianity and especially to the necessity of engaging companies of professional players to perform religious plays for the festival of Corpus Christi, a movable feast which falls roughly two months after Easter, usually some time in June. The players were further bound into the socio-institutional fibre of the Church when, some time between 1565 and 1568, they accepted the patronage of the *cofradías*, fraternities of devout laymen, which provided playing space in exchange for a percentage of performance profits to be used in support of the public hospitals and orphan asylums. In this way the Spanish theatre very early acquired a kind of dual or ambivalent character. On the one hand, plays were seen as an encouragement to idleness and improper passions; on the other hand, they were instruments of Christian instruction and inspiration. On the one hand, players were a gang of libertines and women of no virtue; on the other hand, they served the Church and supported charity with their labours. Virtually every major playwright of the Spanish Golden Age — excepting Alarcón, but including Lope de Vega — took holy orders at some point in his life.

On the one hand, Spanish *comedias* were extremely chaste in language and presentation. The locker-room bawdy of Shakespeare is conspicuously absent from the plays left us by Lope and his colleagues. On the other hand, *loas* or prologues presented before the play and *entremeses* or interludes presented between the acts amply supplied the low and provocative content that delights the masses and outrages the guardians of mass morals. Seductive dances by women were especially popular, and whenever theologians argued for the closing of the theatres, the lascivious *zara-banda* and the enticing *chacona* were singled out for most special disapproval. The ultimate and insupportable conflation of the sacred and the profane, according to some, was the damnable spectacle of a lascivious *zarabanda* being performed by the very actress who had so moved us to spiritual tears as the Blessed Virgin.[11]

But for better or for worse, professional theatre of one sort or another could not be denied the seventeenth-century Spaniard. The meanest and most isolated hamlet would assemble for the single vagabond, or for the ragged bands of two, four, or half a dozen players who roamed all over Spain, playing for bread and soup and a place to sleep for the night. A bizarre description has come down to us of the men carrying the women and the costume trunks along dusty highroads, the women adorned with stage beards to protect their complexions from the hot Spanish sun.[12] It is important to note that the Spanish temper of the time considered it more obscene to have boys playing women's roles (although, women being lacking, they did so) than to have women display themselves on a stage. The line was drawn, however, at actresses appearing skirtless and in tights, "apparelled as men."[13] Often the women could sing or dance. Sometimes the men played musical instruments. Companies were by law required to have licenses, but many, many companies travelled the country without them.

At the other end of the scale from the dusty village representations were the lavish entertainments of the court. Philip IV, born in 1605, about the time *The Steward* was written, would pull actors out of performance to rehearse for his private festivities, which could be miracles of spectacle and expense, with stages floating on lakes and whole theatres erected temporarily in a garden. Noble amateur thespians often condescended to perform likewise in allegories about Beauty and *Amor*, and the performance of a crown prince was bound to be excellent, even if the movement of his Cupid car unseated his digestion.

In addition, all the major cities — Toledo, Segovia, Valencia, Barcelona, Zaragoza, Seville, and, of course, Madrid — had theatres and engaged for plays. The solid centre of the system was supplied by a few licensed professional companies, at one time restricted to four, later expanded to a dozen. The head of the company was a person called the *autor*, not normally an author by Lope's time, but a composite actor/director/producer/manager (usually a male, but sometimes a female), who bought the play, hired the players, contracted with the authorities, distributed wages and shares.

There were, physically, two different types of theatre buildings that served Spanish plays at this time: the closed private theatre and the modified courtyard or *corral* that admitted the general public. The playing areas in both were characterized by the absence of that peculiarity which the eighteenth century institutionalized, the proscenium arch or "picture frame," which contains stage action in a cabin and concentrates the attention of the audience visually. In striking contrast, the audiences of late sixteenth- and early seventeenth-century plays were normally gathered in horseshoe or staple-shaped tiers around a pillared but essentially open stage. Actors entered primarily through doors or curtains from the tiring house which was directly behind the stage, but a great deal of variety was afforded by trapdoors giving access from below, machinery giving access from above, and simple impudence which allowed for forays into and out of the "house," sometimes on horseback to facilitate the parting of the crowd.

Private theatres varied from a simple chamber in the house of a nobleman, where the players of a particular company might be summoned for a special occasion, to the magnificent playhouse of Philip IV in the palace of Buen Retiro, in 1632 the *dernier cri* of splendid stagecraft and Italian design. Productions at court theatres could be (and often were) eye-popping extravaganzas with sets of cathedral opulence and spectacular special effects.

Productions at public theatres, on the other hand, lacking the resources of a court treasury and "turned over" at least weekly, were for a long time much simpler: sets were minimal, effects selective, environment supplied by poetic suggestion. Only costumes defied restraint. Actors and actresses were exempted (onstage) from the sumptuary laws, and staggering sums were spent on apparel, sometimes by the players themselves, sometimes by the *autores*. When money was short, precious costumes could be pawned or sold, and perhaps bought back again when luck improved. In the latter part of his life, Lope had reason to deplore the encroachment of perspective sets and flashy spectacle upon the relatively chaste public theatre. Yet oddly he, like others, attributed what was in fact a gentrification of stage conventions to "the taste of the vulgar."

Public theatres were not only built upon the model of an open courtyard as Shakespeare's Globe was, but often as not were built in, and indeed out of, open courtyards, where the backs of a square block of houses sheltered a cool yard, and rear windows al-

lowed householders and their friends — and others who could pay
— a tremendous windfall. They were, like the characters in the famous Hitchcock film, able to observe neighbouring murders and
love affairs from the comfort of a private apartment — refresh-
ments available. These windows, of course, were reserved for the
elite, and were protected from the low crowd in the yard — since
the theatre drew its audience from all levels of society — by grates
of black ironwork, which were sometimes bellied out to allow the
privileged playgoer to lounge upon the sill. The low crowd in the
yard might stand, or pay extra to hire a seat on the bleachers.
Members of the religious community had a gallery at the back reserved for them, and women — since women formed a sizable and
enthusiastic portion of the Golden Age audience — had another.
Under the women's gallery or "stewpot" there might be a drink
concession, selling a kind of Spanish mead. A canopy roof covered
the stage, but the standing *mosqueteros*, craning their necks to view
the raised stage, had to jostle one another under an open sky.[14]

Public performances were held by law in the afternoon — not
in the morning when they would deter people from mass, nor
after dusk when decent citizens preferred to avoid the street.
Some attempts were made likewise to restrict playgoing to two or
three days a week, but such restrictions could not be enforced for
long. By and large, except during plague, Lent, national mourning, or the heat of summer, Spaniards demanded, and usually got,
plays every day of the week, including Sunday — especially Sunday. The bill was changed every few days, as soon as attendance
dropped. New plays were needed constantly.

In startling contrast to the arrogant, unsmiling aristocrats in
black that many people exclusively associate with this period,
Golden Age audiences were — like their English counterparts
across the water — extremely boisterous and rowdy. But the conduct of Lope's public in the theatre must be seen as manifesting a
definite and widely understood set of conventions. In our own
time we accept a wide range of conventions as appropriate for different circumstances, from the decorum of a "legitimate theatre"
audience to the uproar of the spectators at a rock concert. Opera
audiences are expected to be more vociferous than ballet audiences. In general, however, throughout modern history, audiences
who were passionate lovers of an art, emotional advocates of one
performer over another, have been noisy, and even combative. As
often as not, furthermore, they have been participants in the most
creative and vigorous periods of the art. Therefore, although contemporary chroniclers of the Golden Age seem to concur in

deploring the whistling, stamping, and dragging of keys across the metal window grates, the shouting, hawking, and loud, sometimes violent disputes, even the passionate cries of "*Vitor! Vitor!*" when a performance displayed particular excellence, the theatre in fact flourished in this clamour.[15]

For all the clucking, we must not assume that Lope would have been better appreciated had his audience been more sedate. Aggressive displays of disapproval in this context suggest that aggressive displays of enthusiasm were even more the norm. Furthermore, there may even have been a more specific role for audience noises to play. Flamenco dancing at its most concentrated pitch is supported and sustained by shouts and clapping or by murmurs and comments. True *aficionados* are highly sophisticated about this kind of participation, know when and how to break in, can follow the subtlest rhythm of the performer and serve rather than break his concentration. Pentecostal preaching encourages interjections as well as answers from the congregation. In the realm of popular music, an audience devoted to a particular artist scatters applause for just the right number of bars at the opening of a favourite song, or someone calls, "We love you, Judy!" In all these cases we have an audience that is unusually and intimately involved, following very closely the artistry as well as the emotion. In addition, all of these circumstances involve a performance with a clear and perceivable rhythm which an audience can recognize, adjust to, and respond within. Verse drama is also, albeit more subtly, rhythmic, and we may assume that when a Golden Age audience gave approval to a play and its performers — which most often they must have — that the "boisterousness" was refined into this kind of charged participation and that performers of Lope de Vega's intimate, passionate, and very human plays drew eagerly upon this energy.

The Play

The Duchess of Amalfi's Steward is the work of one of history's greatest dramatic geniuses at the height of his powers. In the vigour and elegance of its language, the vitality and subtlety of its characterizations, the warmth and humanity of its world view, the sheer virtuosity of its stagecraft, it represents the master at his best. As is typical of Lope, all of these elements are addressed to a kind of emotional seduction. Unlike other artists who consciously serve a moral or aesthetic idea, Lope does not dominate, outrage, nor —

at least directly — challenge or instruct his audience. Rather he moves, amuses, excites, intrigues, and beguiles. The vitality of his art is infectious rather than overpowering, as he woos the will of an audience like an artful suitor.

Language

This being the case, it is not remarkable that some of the most beautiful poetry in the play is found in the soliloquies of Antonio, the lover. These soliloquies, furthermore, while always true to the character who speaks them, represent a variety of emotions. The passionate opening soliloquy is *romance*, ballad form,[16] which uses extended patterns of assonance instead of rhyme. Here the speech is structured in stanzas like a song, with a recurrent refrain — "Alas for a humble man!/Pursue the wind and catch fire," — that is typically Lopean: at once evocative and elusive. Midway, this soliloquy modulates very like a musical piece changing key, from a powerful expression of emotion to a meditative recollection of the life leading up to this moment, ending with a return to the original theme and the refrain. Reading (or hearing) a speech like this, one is reminded that Lope was the first of the great playwrights to write an opera libretto.

In contrast to the powerful rush of feeling of the opening speech is the tender lyricism of the brief soliloquy beginning, "Love with frosty wings/bears up my hope" (I. 277 94). This speech is in the versatile *redondillas* (rhymed quatrains) and is almost pure imagery. It in turn contrasts with the exultant paean to married happiness and children (II. 171-210) culminating in "O what children, blessed heaven!/ O what glory! O what gifts!" and patterned in *quintillas* (five-line stanzas, two rhyme endings), slightly larger units allowing here for a looser presentation of images, a less formalized quality. Unlike any of these is the distracted, rhythmically stark and almost imageless soliloquy after Antonio has allowed himself to be separated from his family: "Where does my fortune lead me. . .?" (III. 655-91). The lines suddenly contract from the four-stress pattern of the previous scene. Yet the three-stress pattern, *redondilla* again, is like "Love with frosty wings," whose closing question is:

Ah, who that grasped the fire
of such a love as this
would — for some little pain
it cost him — let it go?

In dialogue as well, Lope is able to make fineness of formal control serve rather than straiten the effect of genuine emotion, at least in part by means of his powerful dramatic sense. Dialogues as different as the courtship scenes between Antonio and the Duchess in Act I, the letter scene between Antonio and Urbino also in Act I, and the lovers' squabble between Doristo and Bartola in Act II give the participants such clear and strong dramatic objectives that we feel mere language cannot contain what they need to communicate to one another. No matter how consciously articulate the speaker, no matter how artful the poetry, language is never the most important thing that is going on; it is irradiated by the dramatic situation, and is merely, as it were, "the vehicle of the soul."

A striking example of this is Urbino's monologue on jealousy in Act II, which can seem on first reading to be both overwrought and overlong. In fact, it is one of the pitfalls of reading what is in essence a theatrical blueprint to lose the situation for the words. What has happened on stage is that a newborn baby has been accidentally handed to a man in a jealous rage, barely in control of himself. Apprehension in the audience is immediate, and builds during Urbino's speech, which is not dramatically the curious academic exercise it in part appears, but rather a device for tightening and tightening the fearful tension as Urbino works himself up to a greater and greater pitch of rage against the helpless infant in his arms. Each stanza is another turn. When Antonio — the child's father — enters, our anxiety is raised yet another turn. Furthermore, Antonio is helpless to act, since any aggression on his part would certainly provoke violence to the newborn Leonora. All he has are desperate, inadequate words. Again language has tremendous importance, and control of it is crucial, not for its own sake, but for the sake of what needs to be conveyed.

In a sense, technical virtuosity with language comes so easily to Lope that we are not invited to be disproportionately impressed by it. Characters such as Antonio and Doristo have the verbal skill to be charlatans, but in fact they are never so enchanted by their own verbal constructs as to lose firm anchorage in reality. Doristo has the impulse to bamboozle in play, but not to deceive in earnest, and Antonio's seminal characteristic is "his truth above all else."[17] It is this melding of the most elegant technical artifice with the most direct emotional urgency that gives Lope's language its peculiarly persuasive power.

Characterization

An extraordinary benignity, typically Lopean in quality, illumines the characterizations in this play. Although he has stayed fairly close to his source in terms of plot, Lope has departed subtly but decisively in conceiving his characters. Despite the assumption by nearly everyone in the story that the burden of the brothers' wrath must fall on Antonio as the interloper and presumably the seducer, other redactors of Bandello take the traditional moral posture of imputing to the woman the greater lasciviousness and an Eve-like role in the downfall of an honest man. Lope discounts the idea of lasciviousness altogether, as well as any trace of seducer/victim dynamics in either direction. In both the Duchess and Antonio physical passion is the force of life itself, the natural expression of affinity and love between a man and a woman. Both lovers are, furthermore, fully and equally responsible. Both woo, and both, in full knowledge of the possible consequences, consent. Indeed, throughout Lope condemns very sparingly. With the exception of Julio and his shadowy minions, there is no character in the play, no matter how minor, that Lope fails to redeem.

The first and primary character for whom he wins our affirmation is the title character, the steward Antonio, whose passionate opening soliloquy seizes us from the outset. An honest, loyal, large-souled man, deeply in love, he engages our sympathy for his torment, our empathy for his passion, our respect for his decency, while he excites and retains our interest with his energy. Antonio's character is crucial to the meaning of the story. He is the measure of the Duchess' error, and it is the audience's evaluation of his worth which to a large extent determines whether she will appear to us as having broken a law or merely a convention. Were he beneath her in anything save rank, the moral, tragic, aesthetic, and psychological possibilities of the story would be quite different.

As it is, it is not only his personal charm that attracts the Duchess, but, unexpectedly, his competence and ability to learn, the fact that he "grasps completely whatever he undertakes." But his central, defining virtue, for the Duchess as well as for the significance of the play, is "his truth above all else." Lope has invested Antonio not only with every moral force and virtue, but with the rounding of dramatic subtleties as well, including humour, eloquence, virility, self-awareness, constancy under pressure, and grace when he has fumbled. In addition, he shows Antonio explicitly as a man who is capable — with a little coaching — of learning a new role and fulfilling it creditably.

In his Duchess similarly, Lope gives us a portrait that is more than merely beautiful and bewitching, although it is surely that. He gives us a psychologically mature woman responsible to several roles, which again are seen as integrated: wife/mistress, mother, and duchess. This Duchess is no fiery individualist, but a woman worthy to be a regent, in whom Christian and secular love are reconciled. In the unity of her personality, responsibility is not seen as adverse to love; rather it is the natural consequence of love. Her care in the education of her son is the same care she exercises in insisting on holy matrimony and in scrupulously discharging her duties to her estate and her servants. But more than that, it is the same care that is manifest in her very sexuality. Granted, Antonio has good looks, social grace, and a great deal of personal magnetism. But it is "his truth above all else" that attracts the Duchess to him. She is a woman who is passionately and physically drawn to integrity. In Lope's lovely heroine, virtue and sexual vitality spring from the same natural source.

In Urbino and Ottavio, on the other hand, the first adversaries of the lovers, Lope shows us the difference between Antonio's ideal love and ordinary romantic obsession. Of the two characters, Urbino is the less attractive figure, so single-minded and mean as to seem blockish, his density a strong foil to the grace, ebullience, vigour, and warmth of the man he thinks is his rival. Humourless himself, he is irresistibly humourous to Antonio, and his worrying of the steward over the Duchess' note provides a scene which is a masterpiece of tension and absurdity. Ottavio, on the other hand, is as entertaining as Urbino is dull. He is the equal of the Duchess in rank, and despite his vanity and affectations, he is no mindless fop. Indeed his wit often borders on self-parody. Antonio accepts him as a worthy suitor to his lady and affords him the highest compliment in this play's vocabulary in calling him "an honest man." Ottavio's fault, like Urbino's, is love corrupted by egotism.

For each of these characters a crucial test is passed when he is required to breach egotism in recognition of someone outside himself. For the limited and dangerous Urbino the other person is the child Leonora, and the breach is brief. Rabid with jealous fantasy, he yet finds himself incapable of harming the helpless infant that is inadvertently handed to him. He steps back on the threshhold of real evil. For Ottavio the other person is the Duchess. From the beginning his love was disinterested enough to disdain financial concerns, but it is not until the end, when he recognizes how his blindness and vanity have colluded with Julio in the final catastrophe, and his reason gives way, that Ottavio is, in some sense, redeemed. His madness seems a purgative one because it involves real contrition for sin, a necessary step towards salvation.

For the fearful Julio there is no redemption. Lope has given him a sudden and baffling inhumanity and such coldness that he does not even know what poison he has given his sister, only how long it takes, as if he had sent a servant to the apothecary and only barely bothered to read the label.

No discussion of Lope's characterizations would be complete without mention of the *gracioso* or comic servant, one of Lope's most popular contributions to stage convention. In this play the *gracioso* is the shepherd youth Doristo, who becomes the foster-father of Antonio's children. It is the *gracioso's* role to comment irreverently upon the central action, but Doristo's role in *The Steward* is more than choric. From an irrepressible boy he matures, act by act, into a good man, Antonio's second, loving generously and loyally and ready to lay down his life for "his" children. In Doristo, too, the bold outlines of a vivid character are softened by shadings of irony, humour, and awareness.

The lovers and their close ally, Doristo, then, are exceptionally attractive figures, exhibiting charm and wit, passion and life, devotion and responsibility. We are drawn not simply to understand them or to identify with them, but to care for them, and this emotional involvement strengthens our perception of their conduct as loving and good. Their lesser adversaries, Urbino and Ottavio, are less attractive, but we are still invited to forgive them and accept them. The moment we forgive them, of course, we concede that their persecution of the lovers is wrong. The avenging Julio, on the other hand, is sudden and repellent, not even allowed the opportunity to become fascinating. By his characterizations Lope wins us to a visceral affirmation of the honest man's right to the woman whom he loves and who loves him.

World View

Despite the grim outcome of the story, what remains with us from *The Steward* in retrospect is the humanity of its vision. From small details of care and courtesy, through the importance assumed by children, up to the abstract considerations of honour and a man's worth, the play draws its power from an unshakable faith in human love as the essential value of this world. The love between Antonio and the Duchess is a generous, generative warmth which embraces not only the children, but, opening outward, comes to include Doristo and Bartola, the palace servants (all of them by the end), Urbino when he learns the truth, and — most crucially — the audience, whose emotional collusion keeps the values of the idyll alive even after the final curtain.

We have noted earlier how the original persecutors of the lovers, Urbino and Ottavio, are redeemed in our eyes. But care is shown for other characters as well. In her climactic revelation speech of Act III, the Duchess clears the reputation of Livia, provides for her estates, and gives her servants free choice of allegiance:

> Any who wish to go
> will have letters and money provided;
> any who wish to remain
> will have a house and my love. (III. 176-79)

No one is forgotten, either by Lope or by the protagonists who are his conduit to the audience. When Antonio leaves the stage with his newborn daughter in his arms, the stage direction does not read merely, "Antonio Exit," or even, "Exit Antonio with the child," but "They exit." Whether or not this suggests that a real infant was used in performance rather than a doll in a blanket, it shows an exquisite courtesy. The Duchess' unborn child is counted by Antonio as a beloved life (III. 666-73). And in her dying agony the Duchess names it — Abel.[18] With the lightest possible touch, consideration is afforded even to Antonio's horse (II. 612-15).

One of the most striking elements of *The Steward* as a love story is the exceptional concern it expresses for children, both as the fruits of love and as beloved in themselves. Indeed the Duchess and Antonio spend as much stage time being parents as they do being lovers, and seem to derive equal satisfaction from both roles. To some extent this represents a Spanish value and a man's pride as *pater familias*. To some extent also it represents a medieval Catholic ideal of woman as madonna. At the very midpoint of the play, like the eye in a storm, is a tender scene at daybreak in which the newborn Leonora is delivered to safety and fostering care in the arms of the peasant Bartola. The Christian evocation of a young woman nursing a child in the presence of shepherd and protective father sheds an emblematic radiance over everything that has happened, everything that is to come. And if we further see the flight of the family in Act III and the slaughter of the children at the end as recalling the Biblical "Flight into Egypt" and the "Slaughter of the Innocents," we are making associations which would have come very readily to an audience which was continually fed with Christian imagery and story, in drama as in other arts.

Moreover, the pastoral world that Doristo and Bartola inhabit is itself a classic convention representing the ideal and the innocent, a convention with which both Lope and his audience were extremely conversant. When Lope makes Antonio the shepherd's lord and friend he further strengthens the association of Antonio with classless human values — Antonio as good father and good shepherd.

Nor is it only infants and small children — easily sentimentalized, perhaps — that are offered as worthy of care. The action is framed, in fact, by the education of the Young Duke, the Duchess' eldest son. On her very first entrance the Duchess is attending to his upbringing. In the very last scene he takes up the terrible responsibilities of manly revenge. That he has been in the interim both lovingly and wisely raised is evidenced by the humanity of his judgement regarding his mother's marriage. The treachery of his uncle is not his fault, but it is his task to "set it right." The murdered family are his mother, the man he has embraced as his father, the children he has accepted as sister and brother. As Doristo was to Alejandro and Leonora, so Antonio was to him. His role is the role of the phoenix, of the parents' love and honour resurrected in the child. To engender, bear, and raise to manhood an honest individual is in this play the task of life fulfilled.

The process by which Lope draws his audience into allegiance with the family of Antonio and the Duchess is a dramatic argument against the code that Julio represents. In this play love is the real basis of honour, and the audience is emotionally persuaded that the lovers act in a way that is right and good. In the end, the unforgivable crime of the play is Julio's. Laying aside his subjective outrage and Ottavio's disappointment, there are no negative consequences to the marriage of Antonio and the Duchess. The laws of inheritance are not violated; the Young Duke succeeds quite smoothly to his father's title and estate. Governance and order are not adversely affected; the Duchess is scrupulously responsible and Antonio is an able and honest administrator. Public morality is not scandalized; the marriage is proper before the law and before God. The essential social hierarchy is not shaken; the Duchess renounces her title and bows to her husband as soon as she may practically do so.

Furthermore, no argument at all is given by Julio in rebuttal. Not only is there no verbal argument — the debate as a whole has not been conducted in verbal terms — but there is no dramatic persuasion in Julio either. Cold, inhuman, without a flicker of conscience in treachery, Julio is in addition a stranger to the audience. We do not meet him until Act III is well underway. Nor does he express even pain, which might win him audience sympathy. Julio possesses not a single persuasive trait dramatically; he merely mouths the code and executes it. Anyone who believed the code would have been free to believe that Julio does what must be done. But anyone vulnerable to Lope's dramatic reasoning would carry away a lingering emotional doubt, a lingering bond with the brief idyll to which he as audience had born witness.

Stagecraft

Lope's seductive power as a dramatist comes not only from his language and his vision, but also from his command of stagecraft and his instinct for what is dramatically persuasive. While he protests himself his public's slave, he reveals himself in *The Steward* to be the subtle and intelligent advocate of a human and moral value system against an aristocratic code. The means by which he wins audience consent to the marriage of Antonio and the Duchess is not, as we have said, the verbal exposition of reasons and principles, but the presentation of character, situation, emotion and humour, carefully addressed to the audience's readiest level of response.

There were many in Lope's audience — his patron the Duke of Sessa for one — who would not have been pleased by the idea that a simple *hidalgo* had the right to marry their sisters, and therefore Lope needed to make his case with extreme diplomacy. Like the English poet Geoffrey Chaucer, Lope was a son of the middle class who rose to become both a versatile and lauded poet, and the factotum of a powerful aristocrat. For a man in such a position there is no virtue so essential as tact. Indeed, when we read Lope we are often reminded of the Chaucerian persona: the charming urbanity, the lightly self-deprecating humour, the exquisite equipoise of tolerance and irony, the evasion of open controversy, the sharpest perceptions smoothed by disarming wit and a tone of almost affectionate good will — an "artless" quality that is the product of consummate art. Beneath the deliberately unthreatening surface, however, in Lope as in Chaucer, are the observations of a man who has crossed classes upward and downward, recognizes the nobility of the plowman as well as the knight, and who knows the world after the particular fashion of one who must be quick in learning, and agile in fulfilling, the peculiar rules of wherever he finds himself. It is no wonder, then, that Lope's portrait of Antonio, the humble gentleman who woos and weds a duchess, is a small masterpiece.

Lope's principal strategy in this dramatic suit being to win us emotionally to the character of Antonio, he begins with the least expected move — straightforward petition. In the very first speech of the play Antonio, alone on the stage, addresses his passion and his anguish not to his mistress or to a confidant, but to the audience. This is no introspective soliloquy accidentally overheard; it is a direct and compelling appeal for compassion. Before the Duchess even appears Antonio has begun his assault on the principal object of seduction — the audience.

The fact that Antonio's is the dominant role of the play, furthermore, insures that it will be played by the strongest male lead of the company, whose personal magnetism and audience following accrue to the character. Lest this seem only the obvious casting for the story, it should be pointed out that Shakespeare's leading man, Richard Burbage, played the avenging brother in John Webster's version. Lope, in addition, knew the contemporary actors and actresses well and, as a playwright whose work was enormously in demand, could choose which company, which players, would best serve his dramatic purpose.

The direct appeal and the magnetism of presence are used by Lope artfully in *The Steward*. A third favoured device is the balancing of amusement and apprehension in an audience, exciting and entertaining while he binds our sympathies to the lovers. We know, for example, that the rules for covering one's head in the presence of the king were, although unwritten and subtle, extremely stringent. Only the highest aristocracy, the *grandes*, could aspire to this privilege of *cubrios*, and within that privilege there were three levels: those who could cover before addressing the king, those who could cover after addressing the king and receiving a response, those who could cover after addressing the king, receiving a response, and withdrawing.[19] Antonio's discomfiture in the business of putting on his hat before the Duchess — whose family were *grandes* — is the discomfiture of a man putting on his hat before a woman whose family may put on their hats before the king. That Lope can bring out both the danger and the absurdity of this transgression is a testament to his virtuosity as a dramatist. That he did so without offending those members of his

audience who took such things seriously is a tribute to the knife-
edge balance of his tact as well.

In this scene the humour in Antonio's sharp situational awareness gives him the colour of a realist and his case the colour of
good sense. This device is used elsewhere in the play to equally
good effect, notably in the letter scene in which Urbino remorse-
lessly presses Antonio to show him the contents of the note the
Duchess' maidservant has passed him. Revelation could mean
death, and Antonio, in desperation, devises the ludic expedient of
relinquishing half the note, letter by letter, in torn pieces. By con-
ducting the whole business as a preposterous game, Antonio urges
Urbino to see how foolish his obsession is. Urbino, of course, does
not. But the audience does. The man obsessed by jealousy may be
dangerous, but Lope emphasizes here that he may be none the less
ridiculous.

Similarly, the comic subplot of Doristo's marriage to Bartola
presents the outraged relative — in this case a sputtering peasant
grandfather — as a figure of fun, who, presented with the reality
of a baby to be born, relents and gives his blessing to the union.
This is the way such a situation is handled in the idyllic pastoral
world; this is the way such a situation should be handled. By first
winning us to the character of Antonio and then showing us
adversaries who are foolishly vain or overwrought, Lope begins to
make his case. Most of the humour is in Act I, however. The play
(in both senses of the word) becomes progressively more dangerous.

Had Lope reduced the roles of Urbino and of the jilted suitor
Ottavio and given us instead more of Julio — his internal conflicts,
for example, over what he feels he must do — it might have been
argued that this play in essence affirmed Duke Julio's code, no
matter how distressing the murders at the end might be. No medieval epic glorifying war, after all, is without strong passages of
grief and dismay at the loss of gallant lives. Yet war is still clearly
perceived as glorious, only the more so because it is painful and
destructive, requiring such strength of will in overcoming natural
human repugnance. The higher the price one pays, the higher the
purpose must be. Lope precludes this line of reasoning by giving
Julio no triumph over softer feelings, by making his role minimal
and arbitrary, by replacing him in visibility by Urbino and Ottavio,
both of whom turn against Julio in the end. It is true that a contemporary might have seen Ottavio's early position as a reasonable
compromise — that Antonio alone should be punished. But Ottavio is, in the end, too ineffectual a character to be standard-

bearer for the message of the play. The diplomat in Lope has covered his rearguard by including this option, but the entire craft of the play builds the argument against it.

Another technique for affirming an unpleasant course of action is presenting it as unavoidable or as preferable to a worse course or to total chaos. Lope eschews this line also. Not only are the lovers and their friends personally attractive, but the idyll they briefly create seems feasible as well as desirable. Throughout the play, moreover, character after character is shown as crossing over to their side: beginning with the maidservant Livia; then (in subplot) Melampo; then the good shepherds Doristo and Bartola; then the first sorting of the servants and Urbino, then Bernardo (marginal, but indicating a kind of "ordinary man's point of view"); then the Young Duke and the second sorting of the servants; and finally Ottavio, whose declaration of the Duchess' innocence and whose intolerable remorse resulting in madness must be seen as a vote cast not only against Julio but in favour of the lovers. In addition, the Cardinal's suggestions that the lovers and their children be punished by banishment seems briefly to have been accepted by all parties, including the aristocrat Ottavio, as reasonable.

By such subtle and seductive means, then, without aggressive pronouncements or "palpable design," Lope woos the audience to care for his characters, to become emotionally involved in their idyll and then, secondarily and almost imperceptibly, to find that they have in so doing espoused a principle which challenges that dimension of the honour code precluding marriage across class lines. Lope himself married once above his class when he first abducted and then (her parents, like Melampo, consenting) wed by proxy the daughter of an ex-*regidor* of Madrid and a royal king-of-arms. And although *The Steward* need not be seen as explicitly autobiographical, it carries a personal urgency and tenderness about it that suggest how much of himself was involved when Lope set out to woo an audience.

Lope and Webster

For English-speaking readers a large part of the interest of *The Steward* must be the fact that it shares a theme with John Webster's *The Duchess of Malfi*, one of the most admired and most performed non-Shakespearean plays of the Jacobean canon. Space will not allow for exhaustive comparison here or even for an exploration of the dramaturgical, theological, and sociological contrasts that immediately suggest themselves, but a few brief critical notes may help to orient the reader coming to this play for the first time from an Elizabethan or Jacobean background, and may suggest ways in which comparative study might be further pursued.

Both Lope and Webster took their plots from a true story narrated in Matteo Bandello's *Novelle*, which Lope was able to read in the original Italian. Webster may also have had access to Bandello, but his main source — although there were several accounts available in English — was probably the one given in William Painter's *Palace of Pleasure*, itself a translation of Francois de Belleforest's redaction of Bandello. One notable difference between Webster's sources and Lope's is that Webster's sources condemn the Duchess as a venal woman whose downfall is caused by lust. Yet the contrasts in vision between Lope's play and Webster's cannot be attributed primarily to differences in their sources. No matter what the judgement of his sources was, everything we know of Lope's life and work suggests he would have been sympathetic to characters motivated to marriage by mutual passion. Nor does Webster's play represent Painter's judgment, but his own.

There are, in addition, a number of parallels between Webster's *Duchess* and Lope's *Steward* which cannot be explained by common sources. In both plays, for example, there is a fear-ridden garden scene at night involving Antonio, a spy that watches him, and a newborn child. In both plays the Duchess is shown the mutilated bodies of her husband and children — in Webster false images, in Lope true flesh. Such parallels have for years stimulated scholars to investigate whether or not Webster might have had access to the Spanish play. The speculation seemed once and for all to have been stilled by the discovery that the actor who played Antonio in Webster's *Duchess* was dead by the end of 1614, while Lope's *Steward* was not published until 1618. Yet *The Steward* had been written by 1604, and in that year relations between England and Spain were officially normalized, Shakespeare's company, the King's men, acting as grooms of the chamber to the Spanish ambassador. Although commerce between Catholic Spain and Protestant England in the three decades following the Armada was certainly neither frequent nor cordial, and although there is absolutely no documentation to suggest how *The Steward* might have become available to Webster, the parallels remain unexplained and tantalizing.

From a critical point of view, however, the contrasts, numerous and striking, reward examination. The first contrast which comes to our attention is that Webster calls his play *The Duchess of Malfi* and Lope calls his *The Duchess of Amalfi's Steward* (or simply *The Steward*). It is an easy error for anyone coming to Lope's play from a close familiarity with Webster's to assume that the Duchess is by necessity the dominant figure in the story. In Lope's version she is not. That is not to deny Camila an important partnership, but Lope has shifted the emphasis, subtly but decisively, to the steward Antonio. Antonio's is the title role and the defining opening monologue. His character is the more challenged and the more complex.

Of course neither of these plays is feminist in any modern sense. Were we inclined to think so, lines in Webster's play such as

> Whether the spirit of greatness or of woman
> Reign most in her, I know not, but it shows
> A fearful madness. . . . (I. i. 504-06)

> I would fain put off my last woman's fault,
> I'd not be tedious to you. (V. ii. 226-27)

> In what a shadow, or deep pit of darkness,
> Doth womanish and fearful mankind live! (V. v. 101-02)[20]

and in Lope's

> She who is highest in rank
> is no prince, nor aspires to be,
> neither serves her own desires
> nor covets liberty. (I. 869-72)

> When a woman's born, a man's ruin begins. (II. 734)

should quickly disabuse us. A bedrock assumption that even a strong woman should be subordinate to her man underlies the thinking of the period and of both these plays. Repugnance against such an assumption should not cause us to distort what is there, either by pretending that these plays are more revolutionary than they are, or by denying that the luminous figure of the Duchess is perfectly *capable* of dominance. When Shakespeare makes Philip the Bastard a better man than King John, for example, he is in no way suggesting that in a better world John would be deposed by Philip. Strong women, like strong retainers or omni-competent valets, can function to support their sagging "superiors" and thus sustain rather than unseat the status quo, as long as honour lies in *resisting* the temptation to rise above one's place. In both plays the Duchess demonstrates exceptional moral force and even sexual initiative, but in neither play does she achieve, or even seek, real equality with men.[21]

What Webster is showing us in his portrait of a duchess who
marries her steward is a diseased world in which everything is out
of joint, distorted, unnatural. A world in which Everyman is a
woman ("womanish and fearful mankind") and her husband is her
underling, impotent every way but sexually, is a world in which
things are not what they should be. However compelling the figure of the Duchess may be, she dies in Act IV, and modern critical
attraction to the intelligencer Bosola is a symptom of the uneasy
sense that the play feels the want of a manly protagonist. The
"womanish" centre of Webster's play is not closet liberalism; it is a
symptom of dis-ease.

What Lope has done in response to the same uneasiness is to
masculinize the play, elevating Antonio to a true protagonist's role
and endowing him with an energy and effectiveness notably lacking in Webster's steward. There is no figure comparable to the
fierce and ambiguous Bosola here because Antonio dominates the
play and our interest. Lope's spies are merely obsessive and self-
involved, beneath the steward in dramatic stature, and the
avenging brother is relegated to the latter parts of the last act. The
world of Webster's play brings to mind the Taoist "feminine" principle, which is called *yin* and assumed to be deep, dark, cold, wet,
passive, and negative. The world of Lope's play is the "masculine"
yang: high, light, warm, dry, active, positive. One need not espouse
such duality to recognize that ideas have often been clustered in
this way.

Entering with his friend Delio, Antonio opens Webster's play
as he does Lope's, and the impediment which will destroy him is
presented immediately:

> You are welcome to your country, dear Antonio —
> You have been long in France, and you return
> A very formal Frenchman in your habit. (I. i. 1-3)

Even though he is home, he appears to be a foreigner. The scene
continues with Delio drawing Antonio out to evaluate by turns the
French court, courts in general, Bosola, the brothers of the Duchess, and finally the Duchess herself. In all of this he is perceptive,
sophisticated, witty — the consummate observer.

He describes the Duchess' excellence to Delio with enthusiasm, but still without express reference to his own feelings:

> I'll case the picture up: — only thus much —
> All her particular worth grows to this sum:
> She stains the time past, lights the time to come. (I. i. 207-09)

The essence of his twenty-two lines is that he admires her greatly, but he seems content admiring, edified by the contemplation of that chastity which "cuts off all lascivious and vain hope."

In strong contrast is the opening of Lope's play. Antonio, alone on the stage, tears into a fifty-line monologue whose self-tormenting refrain, "Alas for a humble man;/ pursue the wind and catch fire!" reveals a man of powerful feeling struggling mightily against it.

Webster's Antonio is removed, passive, maintaining a public decorum. Lope's enters emotionally naked, engaged and fighting. Webster's Antonio admires and we mildly admire him; he withholds aggressive commitment, and therefore he fails to elicit any strong emotional commitment from an audience. Lope's Antonio is so involved and passionate that we cannot help being involved with him; he seizes the audience from the first and makes it his own. Compare the neutralizing playfulness of

> Whilst she speaks
> She throws upon a man so sweet a look,
> That it were able to raise one to a galliard
> That lay in a dead palsy. . . . (I. i. 194-97)

with the implication of this look made personal and explicit:

> But she gave me license, and I dared:
> with looks she summoned me,
> and love has a lynx's eyes.
> Though she spoke not a word to me
> her eyes have told me much.
> It is she who has made me love
> the divine impossible. (I. 20-26)

There is yet another important element which these two introductory scenes contrast, an element first suggested by the English Antonio's use of the word "lascivious" as he insists on misunderstanding the Duchess' "sweet" look, whose meaning is so painfully clear to his Spanish counterpart.

> . . . but in that look
> There speaketh so divine a continence
> As cuts off all lascivious and vain hope.
> Her days are practis'd in such noble virtue
> That surely her nights — nay more, her very sleeps —
> Are more in heaven than other ladies' shrifts. (I. i. 198-203)

Antonio's confusion of sexuality with lasciviousness, celibacy with holiness, is thematic. Indeed, the attitude towards sex in *The Duchess*, like many other elements in that play, is not so much ambiguous as ambivalent. It shifts back and forth between sex as natural and innocent and sex as lurid and depraved. Full of salacious innuendo and imagery, club-footed with sub-plot and incidental characters whose masque is always of lust and corruption — both moral and physical — Webster's play struggles from the beginning to apotheosize the Duchess as an innocent. But the definition of innocence for a passionate woman is a hard time coming, and even when it comes seems more a crown for her enforced penance and almost medieval martyrdom than for the sinlessness of her original conduct. It is part of the play's deep uneasiness, then, that Antonio should insist at the outset on the sexless character of the Duchess' virtue. I do not wish to bear too heavily on what is on one level merely a conventional encomium. The idea that a virtuous woman is vacant of sensual inclination was not invented by Webster. I only mean to suggest that the suspicion of revulsion for a woman's sexuality which peeks out of Antonio's "lascivious" is a filament of a major theme in John Webster's play, namely the imagination of sex as corruption — and that this theme contrasts sharply with Lope de Vega's treatment of the same plot motivation.

The Antonio of *The Steward* has no sexual disgust. His passion is "impossible" but he never thinks he defiles his lady by desiring her or that she is lubricious in desiring him. Nor is he indignant that Ottavio de Medici should aspire to his Duchess. It is natural that he should. Sexual desire is the life force itself. There are problems with its consummation, of course, but Lope's vision is so unquenchably vital that, however Catholic he might be, it is unthinkable in his play that sex itself might be repellent, or that a woman might be more dazzling dead.

It is not only sexuality which shape-shifts in Webster's play. Reality itself twists into masque, echo, nightmare, wax image, lie, replacement, irony, and enacted metaphor. It is Ferdinand, the "sleepless" dreamer, who generates the nightmare which is the world of the play. He is both its victim and its purveyor. The Duchess and Antonio struggle not merely against him, the Cardinal, and Bosola as particular antagonists, but against the nightmare vision, a pervading and demonic irreality which undermines not only any attempt at action, but any assertion of identity and hence of integrity. Individuals are isolated by it, rendered helpless, pressed to despair. The apex of triumph for Webster's Duchess is the insistence that she is sane, that she is real, that she knows who she is.

Because Lope's focus is not on the avenging brother, but on Antonio, the central vision of the play is generated not by a tormented madman, but by a trustworthy, reasonable, and loving individual. God is still in heaven (not merely the stars) in Lope's believing world, and reality is concrete. Identity is not assailed.

Real bonds and stable roles are built. The lovers and their children are treacherously ambushed, but they are never morally isolated, never helpless before an indifferent universe, never overcome by despair. The dream here is not a torturing hallucination, but a willingly chosen idea, a pastoral ideal of human love and community which is briefly, luminously — but truly — realized.

Verse and Translation

I have worked from the text of the Real Academia Española *Obras de Lope de Vega*, volume XV. The line numbering is my own for convenience in reference, the English translation corresponding — with some small flexibility in rearrangement — to the lines of the original text. I have, except in the case of the comic peasants, restricted my vocabulary to terms and idioms which the *Oxford English Dictionary* notes as having been in use in the seventeenth century and which continue to be used in spoken English.

Of primary concern in my translation has been the recognition that *The Steward* was meant to be a spoken text. That this was indeed the contemporary conception of a play is emphasized by the fact that censors did not pass a *comedia* simply from the manuscript, but required to hear it through in private performance. The written word alone was insufficient. Furthermore, Lope repeatedly distinguishes his plays from his other work and insists that they were written quickly and not meant to be pored over in a study.

To some extent this airy posture is a defense against criticism, but in another regard it is simply a statement of fact. Dashing off work white hot is one technique of composition, and indeed one which served Lope exceptionally well. The lengthy literary epics over which he laboured are often an equal labour to the reader. Swift composition was, in addition, a particularly effective technique for producing dialogue that was meant to be spoken. When we remember that the Italian *commedia dell'arte* was in its prime a theatre improvised by the actors around a prepared scenario, we may be further persuaded that Lope's playwrighting technique might have been similar — and similarly legitimate, the primary difference being that the playwright improvised all the roles in his mind and wrote the words down.

This is not to suggest that Lope did not revise. We are fortunate to have autograph manuscripts, and they show that he did. And certainly not *all* his plays were polished off in twenty-four

hours. Nor is it to suggest that in reading his plays we must accommodate carelessness. In fact, *The Steward* is an extraordinarily careful and controlled work. It is merely to suggest one of the distinctive
qualities of Lope's verse: the impression of fluency, immediacy,
the spontaneity of the spoken word.

Methods for reproducing such a quality are bound to be in
large part ineffable, but one important decision I have made has
been to break up syntactical units as they sounded most natural in
English, often eschewing the conjunction *for* and various particip-
ial dependencies. The rhythms of flow and pause are crucial. Sec-
ondly, in translating figurative language I have taken account of
an idiosyncrasy that numerous scholars have noted, that many of
Lope's images, striking and evocative on first hearing, are revealed
in literal translation to be not quite logical, indeed to make no
sense. The effect is similar to that of Impressionistic paintings
which up close appear as daubs of unintegrated colour, but if one
stands back so the eye (or in Lope's case the mind) can meld them,
the impression is of sunlight on a meadow, with the play between
the brushstrokes (in Lope's case the looseness between the images)
lending a kind of shimmer and vivacity. In such cases I have —
like Lope — defied syntactic logic, adjusted particles, and at-
tempted rather to place images in such relation to one another
that they "work" as Lope's do.

Concomitant with these effects of spontaneity is the discipline
of Lope's elaborate verse patternings and metrical virtuosity. Because the imperatives of rhyme would cause the sacrifice of other,
more essential elements; and because rhyme places emphasis on
the words that are rhymed — disproportionately in English, in
which rhymes are comparatively rare; and because one cannot, of
course, rhyme the same words in English as Lope does in Spanish,
I have avoided rhyme. I have, however, recognized where Lope's
prosody places the emphasis in a line and have tried wherever possible to reproduce these emphases in other ways.

There is no standard verse line in Spanish drama that is comparable to Shakespeare's iambic pentameter. It has been said, in
fact, that as a dramatist Lope used every verse form that existed in
Spanish at the time. To essay to reproduce all his prosodic intrica-
cies in an English translation would be a vain obsession. What I
have tried to retain, however, is the underlying sense of musical
patterning that verse gives to dramatic language. Therefore, I
have, in a very simplified way, kept the rhythmic structure of the
lines. That is, in the first section of the play the lines have three
main stresses each (the 3 in parentheses in the left margin indi-

cates this). The three-stress line continues until Antonio declares his love (line 822), where Lope subtly modulates to a four-stress line (again, the number in the margin signals this). Back to three-stress for the continuing dialogue, and then, when the Duchess declares herself (line 901), a sudden expansion to a five-stress line.

This five-stress line, which is most like the Shakespearean line we are used to, is actually used very sparingly by Lope. The most common line is that of the *romance*, the ancient ballad form. In Spanish it has usually three stresses, but eight syllables. Although neither in history nor in prosody is the Spanish *romance* identical, it may be helpful for the English-speaking reader, in listening for the underlying music of *The Steward*, to recall the ballad form in English, its use in charms and nursery rhymes as well as in haunting narratives like "Sir Patrick Spence," "Lord Randal," "Edward," and "The Three Ravens," that rely heavily on dialogue for dramatic force. Chaucer and the English pageant plays, and the Irish plays of W.B.Yeats all share the seemingly artless, deeply emotional song that underlies this play.

NOTES TO THE INTRODUCTION

1 F. de Herrera Maldonado, *Libro de la vida del V. Bernardino de Obregon*, quoted in H. Rennert, *The Life of Lope de Vega* (New York, 1968), 2 and note.

2 This thesis is thoroughly and persuasively argued in A. Trueblood's *Experience and Artistic Expression in Lope de Vega: The Making of* La Dorotea (Cambridge, MA, 1974).

3 F. de Quevedo, "*Aprobación*" to the *Rimas de Tomé de Burguillos* (1634), quoted in J. Fitzmaurice-Kelly, *Lope de Vega* (New York, 1902), 27 and also in H. Rennert, *Life*, 391. *Tomé de Burguillos*, a rhymester in love with a washerwoman, was a character Lope invented for himself when he entered poetic "jousts" which he in his own name administered.

4 Lope refers to *Gran Memoria* in the Prologue to Part XIII of his *Comedias*, quoted in H. Rennert, *Life*, 272. The incident related here is mentioned by J. Fitzmaurice-Kelly, *Lope*, 43 and the plagiarist is identified by name, Ramírez de Arellano.

5 Quoted in H. Rennert, *Life*, 203.

6 *Obras Sueltas*, vol. 1, 285, quoted in Ibid., 139.

7 J. Fitzmaurice-Kelly, *Lope*, 62.

8 R. Rudder, *The Literature of Spain in English Translation: A Bibliography* (New York, 1975), 237-42.

9 Lope's authorship of *La Estrella de Sevilla* has been questioned by some scholars.

10 S.G. Morley and C. Bruerton, *The Chronology of Lope de Vega's Comedias* (New York, 1940), 356.

11 Anonymous, *Diálogos de las comedias* (1620), quoted in H. Rennert, *The Spanish Stage in the Time of Lope de Vega* (New York, 1909), 264.

12 A. de Rojas, *Viage entretenido* (Madrid, 1972). Rojas had himself been a travelling player, and the *Viage*, in the form of a conversation among four actors, is an important source on the pre-Lopean sixteenth-century theatre. A translated excerpt is included in A.M. Nagler's *A Source Book in Theatrical History (Sources of Theatrical History)* (New York, 1952) which, although but meagrely representing the Golden Age, provides several important excerpts on performances and audiences. H. Rennert also supplies contemporary accounts in the last chapter of *The Spanish Stage*.

13 According to the decree of Philip III issued in 1603. In 1615 another decree further stipulated that women were not to appear only in petticoats, but were required to be fully covered. The decrees appear to have had only brief success.

14 J. Allen, *The Reconstruction of a Spanish Golden Age Playhouse* (Gainsville, FL, 1983) gives a thorough and detailed description of the *Corral del Príncipe* in Madrid with illustrations, diagrams, and photographs of a model.

15 See A. Nagler, *Source Book* and H. Rennert, *Spanish Stage* (note 11 above) for contemporary accounts.

16 The *romance* need not be broken into stanzas but can continue for any number of lines, passing from one scene into another. Lines are usually eight syllables (but only three stresses) long. Assonance binds the last two syllables of even-numbered lines. See this introduction, 32-33.

17 It is interesting in this regard that *La verdad sospechosa (The Suspect Truth)*, a play about a brilliant compulsive liar, once thought to be by Lope, is now known to be by Alarcón. It was later adapted by Pierre Corneille as *Le Menteur (The Liar)*.

18 Act III, line 987 and note 28.

19 L. Pfandl, *Introduccion al Siglo de Oro (Cultura y costumbres del pueblo espanol de los siglos XVI y XVII)* (Barcelona, 1929), n. 101.

20 J. Webster, *The Duchess of Malfi*, ed. J.R. Brown (Cambridge, MA, 1964). All quotations from Webster refer to this edition.

21 There was a long (if not dominant) literary tradition of the woman as sexual aggressor, sometimes a demonic figure, but not always. W.S. Merwin's *From the Spanish Morning* (New York, 1985) contains translations of some pre-Lopean ballads on this theme. In Lope's own time Maria de Zayas y Sotomayor developed the type in her *Novelas ejemplares y amorosas o Decame-*

rón español. Her work was praised by Lope, but to my knowledge it is not currently available in English.

BIBLIOGRAPHY

Besides the works mentioned in the notes to the introduction, the following should be mentioned.

Boklund, G. The Duchess of Malfi: *Sources, Themes, and Characters.* Cambridge, MA, 1962.

Brownlee, M. "Belleforest's *Histoire tragique* II, 19 as Model for Lope's *El mayordomo de la duquesa de Amalfi*: A Note on the Poetics of Adaptation." *Critica Hispanica,* 31 (1981), 17-20.

Chaytor, H.J. *Dramatic Theory in Spain.* Cambridge, 1925.

Gasparetti, A. *"Giovan Battista Giraldi e Lope de Vega." Bulletin hispanique,* 32 (1930), 396-97.

Loftis, J. *"The Duchess of Malfi on the Spanish and English Stages." Research Opportunities in Renaissance Drama* 12 (1969), 25-31.
————— "Lope de Vega's and Webster's Amalfi Plays." *Comparative Drama,* 16/1 (Spring 1982), 64-78.

Matulka, B. "The Tercentenary of Lope de Vega: His International Diffusion." *Spanish Review,* 2/27 (1935), 93-102.

Moore, D. *John Webster and His Critics: 1617-1964.* Baton Rouge, LA, 1966.

Potter, L. "Realism Versus Nightmare: Problems of Staging *The Duchess of Malfi.*" In *The Triple Bond: Plays, Mainly Shakespeare, in Performance,* ed. J.G. Price. University Park, PA, 170-89.

Rabkin, N. ed. *Twentieth Century Interpretations of* The Duchess of Malfi: *A Collection of Critical Essays.* Englewood Cliffs, NJ, 1966.

Shergold, N.D. *A History of the Spanish Stage from Medieval Times until the End of the Seventeenth Century.* Oxford, 1967.

Wilson, M. *Spanish Drama of the Golden Age.* Oxford, 1969.

Vega Carpio, Lope Félix de. *Obras de Lope de Vega,* 15. Madrid, 1913.

THE DUCHESS OF AMALFI'S STEWARD
(El mayordomo de la duquesa de Amalfi)

a verse tragedy

DRAMATIS PERSONAE

ANTONIO BOLONIA, steward to the Duchess of Amalfi

CAMILA, DUCHESS OF AMALFI

OTTAVIO DE MEDICI, suitor to the Duchess

URBINO, secretary to the Duchess

LIVIA, maidservant to the Duchess

CELSO, an old servant to the Duchess

DUKE OF AMALFI, son to the Duchess by the late Duke

MELAMPO, an old peasant

DORISTO, a young peasant

ARSINDO, an old peasant

BARTOLA, a young peasant woman

ALEJANDRO, son to the Duchess and Antonio, about 8

LEONORA, daughter to the Duchess and Antonio, about 6

JULIO DE ARAGON, brother to the Duchess

FURIO
DINARCO
FILELFO
RUPERTO
} servants to the Duchess

BERNARDO, a gentleman, friend to Antonio

FABRICIO, servant to Ottavio de Medici

FENICIO, servant to Duke Julio de Aragon

LUCINDO, servant to Antonio

SOLDIERS "with arqucbuscs and halberds"

ACT I

*Number in left margin indicates the number of stresses in a line. See Introduction, pp. 37-39 for a discussion of the verse in this translation.

(3) *ANTONIO: Common, unworthy man!
You aspire to the sun itself!
It is fit that you be punished
and watch the earth go dark.
Eyes which have dared to look   5
on brightness inaccessible —
twinned Icarus[1] of my desire,
with base-plumed wings —
fall from that heaven of contentment
where you mounted, without strength to stay,   10
fall into a sea of tears,
and there let my hopes expire.
     Alas for a humble man —
     pursue the wind, and catch fire.
My eyes have been too free,   15
and have sought the Duchess of Amalfi.
A common man, her hireling,
a man who serves in her house,
I have gazed on heaven's own light
But she gave me license, and I dared: 20
with looks she summoned me,
and love has a lynx's eyes.
Though she spoke not a word to me
her eyes have told me much.
It is she who has made me love   25
the divine impossible.
     Alas for a humble man —
     pursue the wind, and catch fire.
Born a gentleman in Naples,
I studied the profession   30
of attendant to the court.
What beginnings to bring such ends!

Her uncle, Fredrick of Aragon,
was Naples' unhappy king;
when he was cruelly deposed   35
I followed him into sad exile.
He found refuge in France. And, wearied,
after a time I came home
to rest myself awhile:
he is rich who is contented.   40
At length the Duchess, being widowed,
and her son still a tender boy,
wrote to me and asked me
to take service in her house.
Little did I dream, although   45
I had her most intimate trust,
that such mad desire as this
would move me to yearn for her.
          Alas for a humble man —
          pursue the wind, and catch fire.   50
                    [*Enter Ottavio De Medici and servants,*
                              including Fabricio]

OTTAVIO: Has Antonio come?
FABRICIO: Yes, my lord.
ANTONIO: Here I am, sir, awaiting your pleasure.
OTTAVIO: To do so, dear friend, is only
             to reciprocate my love.
             Today hope casts off fear.   55
                    Today on foundations of hope
             I intend to lay the first stone
             for a mansion of happiness.
ANTONIO: [*Aside*]
             I fear very much what he means
             is a marriage to the Duchess.   60
OTTAVIO: [*To attendants*]
                    Be somewhere else, you people.
ANTONIO: What is it you wish, my lord?
OTTAVIO: Attend me.
ANTONIO: I do, my lord.
OTTAVIO: Antonio, I know who you are.
             Do you know me?   65
ANTONIO: Yes, my lord.
OTTAVIO: Then you know that I am nephew
             to His Grace, the most eminent Duke
             of Florence.

ANTONIO: Nay, I know you better:
you're an honest man.
OTTAVIO   I inherit . . . .

Well, I'll have a figure shortly.   70
     Ever since the death of the Duke —
the Duke of Amalfi, that is —
although he left an heir,
I have bethought me, Antonio . . .
ANTONIO: My fears were not in vain.   75
OTTAVIO: . . . to marry my lady the Duchess.
ANTONIO: To tell the truth, my lord,
I am sorry you have bethought that.
Allow me to be candid,
since I only say the truth.   80
     Although my Duchess is
still young and beautiful,
when I yield up her care to a husband
she loses the ward of her son,
and of her estate as well.   85
     Poor and without inheritance,
what will you do?
OTTAVIO: Abide me
by the side of such a woman
as shall bring me untold riches
in the joy of beholding her.   90
ANTONIO: I can well believe, my lord,
it is love that moves you in this,
and a shower of obstacles,
like rain in a hot July,
serves only to increase the heat.   95
     But this heavy weather will pass
and after a month of breakfasts
your soul will be calm again.
Then you'll know what it is to rue
a season's willful madness.   100
     Retired in penury
to some little town where no one
ever comes to see you,
you will find consequences cooling
the ardor your soul feels now.   105
     Then a just repentance
will spoil your palate so,
that you will cease to crave.

	For love's delight, my lord,
	is a kite upon the wind.	110

OTTAVIO: I have not summoned you, Antonio,
to solicit your advice
when my mind is already made up.
Nor are you so old and sage
as to know better than myself.   115
It is only as you are her steward
and privy to her mind
that I wished to inform you of my suit.
It never crossed my thoughts
that you stood to lose so much.   120
But, of course, if it deprives you
of control of her estate,
why, you do well to oppose it.

ANTONIO: It ought not to cross your thoughts
that for the sake of self-interest   125
I would compromise what I am.
I did not come here to serve
from self-interest, but from the affection
which I have maintained all my life
for the house of Aragon.   130
I am poor, perhaps, but not
so poor I am dependent
on the Duchess' estate.

OTTAVIO: You surprise me,
Antonio, and I regret
that my holy and honest love   135
is seen in an ill light by you
if you get no advantage from it.

ANTONIO: Advantage! Enough, by God!

OTTAVIO: What is it to you if she
and I live poor hereafter?   135

ANTONIO: Nothing at all. Go marry.
Marry twenty times over.

OTTAVIO: Antonio,
this is true love. You see that.

ANTONIO: It must be. What else in this world
makes a man commit such folly?   145

OTTAVIO: And will you tell her so?

ANTONIO: I will serve you in this, my lord.

OTTAVIO: If you might persuade her of it.
How I. . . .

ANTONIO: I said I will.
                     I will serve you in this. Godspeed.   150
                     You have my word as a gentleman.
                     If I have any influence with her
                     I shall use it to plead your suit.
OTTAVIO: And I shall repay you, Antonio,
                     if I succeed in it.   155
                          You shall have a guerdon, Antonio,
                     a chain of pure gold, worth a thousand
                     escudos.
                                                      [*Exit Ottavio*]

ANTONIO: I have no choice
                     but to labour in your cause.
                     Why, eyes, do you fill with tears?   160
                          Why not weep me an ocean, then,
                     where I can drown myself?
                     Fie, what an ingrate, Antonio!
                     I should be thankful for this: 165
                     'tis a spar to rescue me.
                          Once the Duchess is married
                     this futile love's vain longing,
                     this insane desire, must die —
                     if an effect will die
                     when the cause is plucked away.   170
                          Or else I'll know her mind
                     regarding marriage. O,
                     take heart, mad little hope,
                     so puny a thing that boldness
                     is dismayed to look on thee!   175
                                                     [*Exit Antonio*]

                          [*Enter the Duchess of Amalfi in
                          widow's weeds; Livia her maid; and
                          Celso, an old man*]
DUCHESS: Where is the Duke, my son?
CELSO: At his lesson, madam.
DUCHESS: Which lesson?
CELSO: Now that he can write   180
                     he is prepared to commence
                     with the study of grammar.
DUCHESS: Good.
                     He should know Latin at least,
                     as will befit a prince.

CELSO: He recites so well, my lady,   185
              he will soon be done with that, too.
                    His Excellency is, I think,
              the child with the liveliest mind
              in all of Italy.
DUCHESS: It shows that he was well sired.   190
                    Go and tell his tutor
              he is not to neglect use of arms.
CELSO: The ornament of letters
              and a skillful swordsman, too!
                    By my faith, if I could shake   195
              some several years from my back,
              I should teach him more of arms
              than Rodomont[2] himself.
DUCHESS: Why, were you a swordsman?
CELSO: Ay,
              and no equal in all Italy.   200
              But now, to my misfortune,
              this staff is the better fencer:
              it has me quite fenced in.
DUCHESS: Go do as I bid you.
CELSO: Yes, madam.
                                            [*Exit Celso*]
DUCHESS: Ah, Livia! What care
              this love costs me!   205
LIVIA: And me
              no less, though I am free,
                    to see you so vexed and troubled
              over someone so far beneath you.
              Why, if you suffer human frailty,
              how shall I fare when my turn comes?   210
                    I am free, but I see full well
              how you chafe to destroy yourself.
              It is an ill thing for a woman
              to be widowed in her youth.
DUCHESS: Why, Livia, do you imagine   215
              that for mere human frailty
              I am willing to offend
              first God, and then my honour?
LIVIA: Then why have you sent for the steward?
              What will you say to him?   220
DUCHESS: I think you know that already.
LIVIA: Your life will pay the forfeit

for this unseemly marriage.

DUCHESS: You love him yourself.

LIVIA: I, madam?
May heaven strike me down   225
if ever I think such a thought!

DUCHESS: I have trusted you greatly, Livia.
I have shared my soul with you.

LIVIA: Prove me however you will.

DUCHESS: Whatever secrets I have   230
are already yours. I have told you
what I dared not tell myself.
And if I briefly imagined
that Antonio reigned in your heart,
it is only because his mind,   235
his person, and his spirit
would kindle love, I think,
in the iciest resolve.
So well-spoken a man! So handsome!
How well he writes, and grasps   240
whatever he undertakes.
How can you not admire him?
His fine manners, Livia. Tell me,
are you not amazed
by his truth, his honest bearing,   245
his noble and impeccable dress —
but his truth above all else?
How well he sets his spurs
to a horse! How well he sings!
What grace!

LIVIA: I am more amazed
by this rhapsody of yours!   250
But if some malignant star
eggs you on to such folly, madam,
that you lay down your pomp and power
for a steward to trample on,
at least, pray you in God's name,   255
take some care for your honour's secret.

DUCHESS: Marriage will shut the door
to all vain trepidation.
It shall be performed in secret
and by the time it is found out,   260
well, they will find I am his wife.

LIVIA: I should say, rather, his death.

I don't know. I tremble for you.
I neither encourage nor impede you.
But if you crave a husband,   265
there are many with a craving for you,
    if not of your own rank,
little less.

DUCHESS: I am well aware
that to marry my servant gainsays
the authority of my rank.   270
    But I trust in secrecy,
since for us to be married
is more than respect for my honour;
it is proper fear of God.
It will not be found out if I trust   275
only you and him.

LIVIA: God grant it.

                                        [*Enter Antonio*]

ANTONIO: Love with frosty wings
bears up my hope — a moth
    borne upward to the flame —
to the sun of those bright eyes!   280
Who calls himself worthy of them
has the pride of Lucifer.[3]
    I go where I must burn.
But everything natural wills
that her beauty must make me bold   285
and give me the strength to succeed.
    The satyr that saw the flame
grabbed hold with both his hands —
but, when it burned him, he cried
and flung it away again.   290
    Ah, who that grasped the fire
of such a love as this
would — for some little pain
it cost him — let it go?
    . . . Is the Duchess here?   295

DUCHESS: Antonio!
ANTONIO: My lady!
I wish to speak alone
with Your Excellency.

DUCHESS: So.
Then, Livia, wait without.
I pray you, clear the chamber.   300

ANTONIO: Sweet heaven! I am blind!
LIVIA: Consider your station, madam.
                I pray you, come to yourself.
DUCHESS: Go. Say no more.

                                        [*Livia exit*]

            [*To Antonio*]
            Why do you look so amazed?
ANTONIO: To find myself here, my lady.
DUCHESS: Have you not been here before?
ANTONIO: Never on such an errand
            as I have on this occasion.
            It is that which unnerves me, madam.   310
DUCHESS: Unnerves you, Antonio? Why?
            Am I so impatient and sharp?
ANTONIO: [*Aside*]
            Say rather so beautiful:
            I tremble before your beauty.
DUCHESS: Although as I am your mistress   315
            I may inspire some fear,
            yet is not a woman's mildness
            enough to allay it again?
                Have I a fearful temper?
            Am I haughty? Am I grim?   320
ANTONIO: Your Grace must know already
            what it is that makes me afraid.
                If a man draws back a curtain
            and thereby discovers an angel,
            does he not rightly tremble
            to behold divinity?   325
                It is not grim things alone
            that we tremble to look upon.
            Great beauty can unman the bravest;
            you may believe me, madam.
DUCHESS: But is it greater now
            than at other times you have seen me?
ANTONIO: Other times other judges came with me
            when you gave me audience.
                When a man stands alone beholding   335
            a more than mortal beauty,
            his judgements, his thoughts, incline
            to some temerity.
                Who can restrain his thoughts?
            For that first, wingéd impulse   340

	which escapes the will is blameless	
	and cannot give offense.	
DUCHESS·	Nor should I, Antonio, be offended	
	if you, as a man, should have thoughts	
	of me as a woman.	

ANTONIO: Just so.   345
          You have read my fear very well.
                    I am grateful to your kindness
          and to your noble discernment
          for this indulgence, madam.
DUCHESS: Come, leave off "indulgence" and "noble."   350
                    Speak familiarly to me.
          Although I am your lady,
          I am not always installed
          on the throne of my tedious title.
                    And although I have been called   355
          by some a discerning woman,
          yet, as for that, very rarely
          is anyone perfectly so.
                    In effect, I have never chosen
          to believe in my own judgement.   360
          A woman's government —
          well, how could it be wise?
                    For that I brought you here.
          And since you have governed for me
          son, house, dukedom, and estate,   365
          with merits that are your own,
                    I wish from this time forward
          that you speak to me otherwise.
          Cover your head.
ANTONIO: Stay, madam.
          Give me leave awhile for amazement.   370
                    Give me leave awhile to prostrate
          my humbleness at your feet.
DUCHESS: Nay, rather speak to me proudly.
          Dispense with courtesies.
                    Cover your head.
ANTONIO: My lady,   375
          if you do me so much favour
          you will make my thoughts more bold
          than they are wont to be.
                    By my faith, I must speak out
          what till now I have kept silent.   380

DUCHESS: [*Aside*]
             I did it. He understood me.
             Enough to look, to listen.
                   Having seen all my soul exposed,
             he has just now understood.
             It should suffice that a woman,   385
             and one as noble as I,
                   has spoken out in such terms.
             Dare then! Why does he hesitate?
             A man has to be a fool
             to keep silent when love speaks to him.   390

ANTONIO: You know, madam, that Ottavio
             de Medici. . .

DUCHESS: What is this?

ANTONIO: . . . that he, full of happy hopes
             (And I hope this does not displease you.)
                   has sent for me today   395
             and requested that I speak to you.

DUCHESS: [*Aside*]
             Why does he bring this up now?
             He can't be in love with me!
                   If, as I have suspected,
             he bears me some affection,   400
             he should know my mind as well
             as if I had spoken out.
                   Without knowing for certain that he loves me
             I can hardly declare myself.

ANTONIO: Either you will not hear me
             or honour deflects you from it.
                   I say, my lady, that Ottavio
             adores Your Excellency.
             He is a man of parts,
             as you know, and wise, and gallant.   405
                   He wishes to marry you, and asks
             no more dowry than your person.

DUCHESS: [*Aside*]
             He brings me Ottavio's suit!
             He's a man. The suit's his own.
             [*To Antonio*]
             Indeed, every man has the right   410
             to declare to the woman he loves
             that he loves her.

ANTONIO: Even so. And Ottavio

	declares it to Your Excellency;	
	and, being your equal, he aspires	
	to make you his wife.	
DUCHESS:	A man	
	who is not my equal offends	
	if his love is an evil one.	
	But can true love be wrong?	
ANTONIO:	No. And yet if love	
	becomes desire, and desire	420
	pleads for the prize of passion?	
DUCHESS:	Before what judge does he plead?	
	Can a man call false witnesses	
	if the lady whom he loves	
	is the judge who decides his case?	425
	I wonder at you.	
ANTONIO:	Why, madam?	
DUCHESS:	Don't look upon my rank.	
	Speak as my head, Antonio,	
	not merely as my steward.	
	Speak to me as a man.	430
ANTONIO:	I cannot.	
DUCHESS:	Why? What's the matter?	
ANTONIO:	I tremble.	
DUCHESS:	From what? What's to fear?	
ANTONIO:	I fear, madam, what could happen	
	if I ceased to fear so much.	
DUCHESS:	Are you cowed by my forwardness?	435
ANTONIO:	No, by God! But tell me,	
	what shall I say to Ottavio?	
DUCHESS:	Listen, and abide the answer.	
	Imagine you are setting out	
	upon a lengthy journey	440
	over land or sea,	
	intending to go alone,	
	when two would-be fellow travellers	
	present themselves at your side.	
	Each for his part will offer	445
	his company to the journey's end.	
	Toward one of these you feel	
	a natural inclination,	
	and in his conversation	
	find amusement and delight.	450
	The other you detest —	

	and that so heartily	
	that just to hear him speak	
	oppresses your spirits quite.	
	With which of these two, then,	455
	would you take up your journey:	
	him you love, or him you hate?	
ANTONIO:	Is there any doubt	
	what the answer is?	
DUCHESS:	Say, though —	
	with which one would you go?	460
ANTONIO:	I would go with the one I liked better.	
DUCHESS:	So I intend to do.	
	Marriage is such a journey,	
	as long as to the end of life.	
	And the proffered company	465
	I imagine as two different men.	
	Ottavio is the one I detest.	
ANTONIO:	And the one you love, who is he?	
DUCHESS:	Have I exposed myself	
	so much and you see so little?	470
	Where are your wits, Antonio?	
ANTONIO:	Blinded by humility, madam.	
DUCHESS:	I must blush to broach the subject	
	of my marrying a second time.	
	But wait here for a note from me.	475
	You shall know the man I love.	

[*Aside*]

                    If his love for me is true,
                    he must know, without notes, who it is.

                                                        [*Exit the Duchess*]

ANTONIO: Cowardly conscience! O,
                   heaven blight your craven hope!   480
                   To come so near the prize
                   and then crumple in humbleness.
                   Then you deserve what you suffer,
                   when you love, and are loved, and dare not.
                        Occasion has a single forelock;   485
                   you must snatch it as she comes towards you.
                   Once past, she is bald behind.[4]
                   What's left? What hope is there?
                   What debt can you dare to claim
                   when you have cancelled this one?   490
                   Ah, sweetness of fair eyes,

hold back my fortune's wheel!
Who hesitates is lost.
Coward! And lost for good!
But her note must tell me so.   495
I deserve this lingering death,
when I had it in my hand!
Love grants no second try,
when it beckons, and you pass it by.

[Enter Livia with a note]

LIVIA: My lady the Duchess told me   500
to give you this note. Here.
Take it.

ANTONIO: If I upset her
by suggesting she marry again
I am deeply sorry, Livia.

LIVIA: She said the note contains   505
the name of the man she loves.

ANTONIO: My only concern was her happiness.
And I thought the house of Medici
was worthy of her rank.

[Enter Urbino, the secretary]

URBINO: She is in love with him!   510
She gave him a note. Stay, Livia.

LIVIA: What is it?

URBINO: I see my suspicions
were right. What paper was that
you gave Antonio?

LIVIA: I?

URBINO: You, madam.
With the tenderest look to attend it.   515

LIVIA: It is true I gave him a paper.
It is false that I gave him looks.
But a man always sees, Urbino,
whatever he chooses to see.
The paper was simply an order   520
of some fabric for a dress.
Good day to you.

[Exit Livia]

ANTONIO: What damned luck
I have brought on this thing from the outset!
Did he see her give me the note?

URBINO: Antonio!

ANTONIO: Secretary! Ah.   525

URBINO:	If a secretary be secret, as a faithful friend should be, may you always find me so. I think that Livia loves you.	
ANTONIO:	Loves me? Why?	
URBINO:	Because she submits to you.	530
ANTONIO:	Submits?	
URBINO:	She submitted a note to you.	
ANTONIO:	Well then I confess; it's true. I do fancy her a little.	
URBINO:	Did you know I've been courting her?	535
ANTONIO:	Ah, now I see your drift. Well, henceforth, she is yours.	

URBINO:	If I agree to accept her
	for the sake of our mutual friendship,
	    I must in no way feel
	that you suffer in giving her up,
	nor must I think your love's discourse
	has exchanged any other things.
	    Has she given you other notes?
		540

ANTONIO:	She has given me nothing but this.	545
URBINO:	If my love obligates you at all, share the contents with me, Antonio. Let us peruse it together — On the Duchess' life, Antonio!	
ANTONIO:	I am sorry you approach this business with such suspicion. By God! My word should be enough. Believe me, I will not go near her.	550
URBINO:	Yet do me one favour, just one, and tear it up, unopened.	555
ANTONIO:	I will tear her from my mind; I will do that for you. Let it suffice for us both that the story ends when it starts, without demanding things that go against principles. I would not wish any woman to think me unchivalrous.	560
URBINO:	It is only the great friendship, Antonio, which you and I have shared (and *of* which I must hope	565

you have had proof by now)
    that obliged me to demand
what you have heard me demand.
But since you choose to deny me   570
in this matter of the note,
    our friendship is at an end.
I am disobliged by you.

ANTONIO: Stay; listen a moment.

URBINO: Sir?

ANTONIO: If I am at liberty,   575
    and we are enemies,
I must fancy Livia again.

URBINO: That you are free to do
since we are no longer friends.
    Love her, and I likewise   580
will wound you some day, Antonio,
in the place nearest to your heart.

ANTONIO: Listen and hear me out.
    If I have refrained from replying
it is only because I consider   585
that when one friend is angry
the other must be in the right.
    And just to let you see
what a gentleman I am
instead of responding in kind   590
I will trade you content for contention.
    Is this the paper?

URBINO: It is.

ANTONIO: Well, I break the seal.

URBINO: What for?

ANTONIO: To look at it; and I promise
that afterwards, you shall see it.   595

[Antonio tear off the piece
with his name on it]

See how briefly I glance at it.
Take it.

URBINO: What did you tear off?

ANTONIO: Seven letters.

URBINO: And what do you give me?

ANTONIO: The paper.

URBINO: I am much amazed
you should be so confident   600
of the secret: it is blank.

ANTONIO: So. Try to crack it, then.
        Come, you are good at ciphers.
           And heaven strike me down
        if it doesn't add up to zero.   605

URBINO: But what are you still holding back
        to torment me with? This isn't all.

ANTONIO: Seven letters.

URBINO: Nothing else?
        No More?

ANTONIO: No more, by God!

URBINO: If ever we shared a soul   610
        when I parted mine with you,
           give me at least the first letter
        of the seven.

ANTONIO: Well, I will give you
        to undeceive you further
        two letters from the end.   615
           Take that one.

URBINO: This is *o*.

ANTONIO: Here is *i*.

URBINO: When you tell me two,
        you must tell me the other five.

ANTONIO: Tell five? That I will not.
           What, am I a clock?   620
        Take two and be content.

URBINO: In God's name, give me the rest!
        I will be your friend forever.

ANTONIO: If the best of friendship lies
        in sharing things equally,   625
        then the most you may ask of me
        is half of these seven letters.
           Take three, and the one left over
         we'll split.

URBINO: Give me the whole thing!
        Damn it!

ANTONIO: We shouldn't wrangle   630
        over something so trivial.
           You have two. See here? Two.
        The *o* followed by the *i*.

URBINO: Is this an *n*?

ANTONIO: An *n*.

URBINO: Are they in order?

ANTONIO: Yes.

URBINO:	But this is *o*.
ANTONIO:	And now you have the four last letters.
URBINO.	If only you would give me the rest!
ANTONIO:	Now you go too far, by God! [*Aside*]

     Sweet heaven! She says "Antonio"   640
is the man she would journey with.
The Duchess says she is mine.
I have given him four letters
which he can in no way construe
or use as an excuse   645
for enmity against me.
     This note has nothing on it
but my name. I am rapt with it.
She loves me. It is quite clear.
She has written my name on this paper.   650
I know full well it will cost
my life if ever her brothers
learn of my presumption.
Still, what better way is there   655
     for a man's life to be spent?
[*Aloud*]
Farewell, Urbino.

URBINO:	God keep you.

                           [*Exit Antonio*]

He is sure I cannot understand it.
"*O, i, n, o*" — 'tis nothing.
     No, wait. Only nothing to *me*.   660
But Livia and the Duchess are Spanish:
the house is Aragon.
And Antonio knows the language.[5]
     "*Oi no*." Ah! "Not today"!
They cannot meet today.   665
But why would she write, "Not today,"
when today she could give him the note?
     But wait. These are only four,
and he has kept three back.
If these four are reversed   670
I have the end of *Antonio*!
     Because the three that are left
have to be *A, n,* and *t.*
Antonio must be the word.

But still, what does it mean?   675
   She brought only the name *Antonio*
written on a paper.
If the letters are not forthcoming,
and if it's some trick to thwart me,
   I throw water on this fire   680
only to raise more smoke —
water and fire and smoke
to make my mad purpose blind.
   The water pours from my eyes,
the fire from my heart, and smoke   685
from my frustration. O,
they'll pay for this levity.
   For I shall watch Antonio's
every move. His passion already
has betrayed his friendship to me,   690
and I know he has not given up.
   I shall tell such ill of him
to the Duchess, though it be lies,
that she shall know forthwith
how disloyal he is to me.   695
   I will thrust him from her house.
I will blacken her trust in him.

                                                 [Enter the Duchess]

DUCHESS: Already the first spark catches
and spreads to kindle my soul,
   and begins to rage so fiercely   700
now that I have declared myself,
that death spies me from afar;
my torments have informed against me.
   But as long as I am married
and my honour does not suffer,   705
for such a love as this
death is an easy bargain.
   Here is Urbino. What is it,
secretary?

URBINO: Has Your Excellency
replied?

DUCHESS: I have entertained,   710
Urbino, a thousand opinions
   concerning this arrangement.
The Duke is still very young.

URBINO: Your brother is concerned with your welfare,
my lady.

DUCHESS: I know. Of course.
URBINO: And with that of his nephew, the Duke.
DUCHESS: I will answer my brother directly.
URBINO: I think he wastes his eloquence
              on this subject, Your Excellency,
                  when he bids you to marry again.
              Are you so opposed to marriage?   720
DUCHESS: It doesn't concern me at all.
              I have no thought of it.
                  And my son is scarcely a reason,
              since he has not reached an age
              where he can make a choice,   725
              or fancy a Medici father.
                  What's more, I don't care to be pressed
              on a matter so closely my own.
URBINO: Yet I think you are shortly to hear
              of a marriage which I anticipate   730
              will take place within your house.
DUCHESS: God save me!
URBINO: I regret to distress you.
DUCHESS: Are you saying that one of my women
              is to marry without my consent?
URBINO: To judge without malice, I think   735
              that the persons are honourable
              and that they mean to marry
              for love.
DUCHESS: I'm sure they do.
              But who is in love with whom?
URBINO: Antonio and Livia with each other.   740
DUCHESS: Did you hear this from him?
URBINO: From both.
              And from my own eyes as well.
              But Your Excellency understands
              I reveal this in confidence.
DUCHESS: I promise to keep your secret.   745
              [Aside]
              But not to keep my patience.
              You saw?
URBINO: Livia slipping a letter
              to Antonio.
DUCHESS: When?
URBINO: Just now.
DUCHESS: You may go, Urbino.

URBINO: But madam,
          Am I not bound to be faithful   750
                    to my office, and to the bread
          I have eaten all these years in your house?

DUCHESS: I know already what has happened.
          The steward is not to blame.

URBINO: Not to blame?

DUCHESS: No.

URBINO: This protection   755
          which Your Excellency extends. . . .

DUCHESS: Leave me, you imprudent fool!
          When you bring such evil reports
                    to my attention in the future
          take care you have better proof   760
          than this.

URBINO: But I have told you
          what I saw, as occasion warranted,
                    since I thought it affronted you.
          And these little love affairs
          are more readily forestalled   765
          if they're caught in the early stages.
                    Antonio is my friend,
          but if he offended Your Excellency
          I'd report of my own father
          what I told you of Antonio.   770
                              [Enter Antonio]

ANTONIO: Estacio sent me to say
          that your carriage is ready, madam.

DUCHESS: I had thought to ride out a little
          from the palace this afternoon.
                    I don't know if I shall.   775
          Secretary.

URBINO: Your Excellency?

DUCHESS: I do not wish at this time
          to arouse my brothers' displeasure.
                    Write that I am not well,
          as the reason I have not written.   780
          Meanwhile I'll arrange some way
          to excuse myself from their plans.
                    I must, one way or another.
          And look you, do not speak ill
          of someone who reports of *you*   785

URBINO: much better than you deserve.
I'll go and compose the letter.

DUCHESS: Have this marriage put off.[6]
Antonio.

                                   [Exit Urbino]

ANTONIO: My lady . . . .

DUCHESS: Antonio,
you mismanage my business grossly.   790
How is it Urbino observed you
receiving my note?

ANTONIO: It was Livia's
fault.

DUCHESS: What is befitting
to my honour, as I am who I am,
has not been observed as it should be.

ANTONIO: *[Aside]*
Well they say that, for a woman,   795
to love and to hate are both
the sunflowers[7] of caprice.
[To her]
Pardon, I mistook your meaning;
I mistook the name you wrote.   800
But I see you committed more
to paper than you did to me.
You gave me a paper heart
with my name in the centre of it,
with my name as the heart of hearts,   805
or so it seemed, my lady.
And it seemed the hand that wrote
those seven letters of my name
was a hand — but I misunderstood —
was a hand that you proffered me.   810
But I see my joy was foolish,
my credence more foolish still.
The word was as blank as the paper,
and inscribed, after all, by a woman.
Ah heaven, if only love   815
had known your name as well —
it was free of duties then —
he'd have written out a bond.
Cruel joke to have written my name;
in mourning for my death,   820
my fortunes are as pale as paper,

and my folly wears inky black.
Is this all of my offense?

DUCHESS: Tis enough, and I detest you.
When I offer you my honour   825
you put it down any place you see.

(4)ANTONIO: That humility held my presumption back,
that I feigned to myself not to know your love,
can that, sweet lady, be my offense —
not vanquishing you in the first assault?   830
I pray to heaven the next man I see
may strike me dead where I stand, Camila.
I pray before another dawn break
that Ottavio shall have you, word and deed.
So you may see how I scorch and burn   835
for not seizing occasion by the hair,[8]
I'll go where you never need hear my name.
Or let the occasion seize me instead;
let her hang me up like Absalom,[9]
to die, as I must with your eyes denied me.   840

(3) DUCHESS: Stay, Antonio.
ANTONIO: Why
do you keep me here, Excellency?

DUCHESS: Patience, Antonio, patience.
ANTONIO: Patience at a time like this?
God smite me!

DUCHESS: Nay, although   845
I begin to suspect from this
that you do love me, Antonio,
you must never treat a noble woman thus.
You see me beside myself;
what could you hope I might say?   850
Was I wrong to think
that you might love me, too?
If your chance is bald behind,[10]
I must think you are the barber.
Or might my arms be poisoned   855
that Ottavio must taste them for you?
Should I, without regard
for reason or reputation,
put honeyed words in my mouth,
as if you were the lady?   860
Speak out. Tell me you love me.
Say you're dying. What, do you weep?

	You must know that ladies feel	
	with women's feelings, Antonio.	
	Be bold. I know you love me.	865
	Well then, make love to me.	
	Heaven has granted to men	
	that they should be always the lords.	
	She who is highest in rank	
	is no prince, nor aspires to be,	870
	neither serves her own desires	
	nor covets liberty.	
	O, fie on thoughtful men	
	with their trembling circumspection!	
ANTONIO:	Fools are very bold,	875
	and bold because they are fools.	
	But if my humility	
	displeases you, good madam,	
	if my eyes have winked and wept	
	before so high a sun,	880
	if I have failed in boldness	
	when occasion beckoned me,	
	if I did not speak what I knew,	
	when I knew your heart was mine,	
	yet here I am, come before you,	885
	the altar of my respect,	
	because I dared discreetly	
	to show you how bold I am.	
	I shall dare to seize your white hand.	
	I shall dare to embrace you, and dare	890
	to make my desire a bee	
	and make your mouth a flower.	
DUCHESS:	Stop!	
ANTONIO:	But didn't you tell me. . .?	
DUCHESS:	How dare you suggest such a thing?	
ANTONIO:	Well, I take off my hat again.	895
	Pardon, Your Excellency.	
DUCHESS:	But this is only turning	
	the same mill around and around.	
	For love there is no circumspection,	
	no force that can silence it.	900

(5)   Antonio, I do adore you, but be advised
that I cannot and shall not love you in this way.
You may not touch me anywhere that honour
may feel an affront. And yet in secret, look you,

you may become my lord if you are discreet.   905
My honour shall be yours: I'll pledge it to you.
Antonio, beloved, so that we may shun dishonour,
and more than that, avoid offense to God,
my consent must be to proper marriage only.
And even so, if my brothers should learn of it,   910
I do believe my life and yours are lost.
We'll find no friends in those two highborn men,
whose deeds all France and Spain, and all the lands
washed by the circling oceans celebrate.
Love can be broken by its cause — that is,   915
the yearning lovers have to know each other.
Well, when a child appears we'll have no choice.
We'll say you are my husband. But meanwhile,
(if heaven deigns to grant me so much grace)
a blessed, secret joy of one another   920
is all the consummation I desire.

ANTONIO: This is right, great lady, and honourable.
But I have further reasons of my own.
When I have got the moon of your bright heaven,
shall I not cherish and guard it jealously   925
and keep my good fortune close? By all that's
                                  precious,
not a living soul shall know my lady loves me.
Today you have shaped me and made me. And who
                                  but heaven
can make a man? Nay, who but one by whose grace
I live, could make me worthy? I, your husband? 930

DUCHESS: Ascendant Antonio, from this day forth your star
shall eclipse rank and degree, and I am yours.
All we need find now is a way to accomplish it.
I have still found no means for us to be married in
                                    secret.

(4) ANTONIO: If it is talk you fear, sweet treasure,   935
that some rumour may slander your good name,
I have peasants that live on my estate,
and simple shepherds who tend their flocks.
If you will, we can disguise ourselves
and mingle with them for some little while,   940
and by and by, when we are familiar,
the village priest, knowing us by sight,
may marry us. And then I shall
go mad, I think, that such glory is mine!

DUCHESS: Excellent stratagem! We can leave   945
             tonight, and dress in peasant clothes.
             I shall dress as a page on the road with you[11]
             till we come, dear friend, to that happy place
             where within the honest bond of marriage
             you and I, blamelessly, may have joy of each
                                                        other. 950
ANTONIO: But how shall we explain your absence?
DUCHESS: I will have Livia tell the house
             I am sick in bed.
ANTONIO: Ah. Well prescribed!
             And when night is midway in its course
             and only the great stars light the world,   955
             in the slumbering hour of the deepest dreams
             we'll take two horses and slip away.
DUCHESS: Then go and get them ready.
ANTONIO: And clothes —
             I'll arrange for them, too.
DUCHESS: Oh, all love asks
             is to gain the shore. The water is wide.   960
             God go with thee, sweet lord.
ANTONIO: My love.
(3) DUCHESS: Trust none of my servants, no one.
ANTONIO: Love and I go alone: he will guide me
             and light my way back to you.
DUCHESS: Ah, Antonio, how I adore thee!   965
ANTONIO: May fortune be equally fond.
DUCHESS: Death is nothing, if I die for thee.
ANTONIO: No,
             such death is life.
DUCHESS: Beloved!
ANTONIO: Refulgent bride, God keep thee!
DUCHESS: God bring me joy of thee.   970
                          [Exit Antonio and the Duchess]
                     [Enter Melampo and Arsindo, two old peasants,
                                        and Doristo, a youth]
MELAMPO: Don't stand in the way, Arsindo.
             I'm going to kill this scoundrel!
ARSINDO: Now, Melampo, be more loving.
DORISTO: He's going to kill me? Oh, wonderful.
             Calm down now, Gramp.
MELAMPO: Heaven smite you
             and blast you, and punish you!   976

DORISTO: Now Gramp, just calm down.
               Now listen. Calm down, Gramp.

MELAMPO: Is this the respect you show me?

DORISTO: What respect should I show you?   980

MELAMPO: You'll see, you young whelp, you'll see!
               You are making a grave mistake!

ARSINDO: May I know what's going on?

DORISTO: I just want to get married, that's all.

MELAMPO: He just wants to tread the chicken   985
               before he's out of the shell.
               I married his mother off
               when she was forty and ready.

DORISTO: If she could hear you say that,
               she'd cry false, I swear.

MELAMPO: How's that?   990
               Was this in some foreign country?
               Are you calling me a liar?

DORISTO: No, Gramp. It's just that all women
               get married when they're fourteen.
                  So if she was fifteen, say,   995
               and now she's forty, she says thirty,
               which is more than fifteen, but she adds
               fifteen years to seem younger, but she's not.
                  And if she has a daughter
               and the daughter is ready to get married,   1000
               her mother will say she's fifteen,
               because if she said twenty, she's fifty.
                  Fifteen and fifteen totalled
               would make her thirty.

ARSINDO: That's true.

DORISTO: But we don't have to go that far.   1005
               Because at fifteen Mom was married,
                  she would certainly say
               that now that I'm fifteen, too. . . .

MELAMPO: Shut up, Doristo, dammit!

DORISTO: That would make her past thirty now.   1010
                  Well, there's all kinds of crazy ways
               you can wrangle to deny her age,
               but common sense will tell you
               that years are like sins, you know,
                  and they show in a woman's face.   1015
               It's silly to say they don't.
               But in order not to confess them

nobody confesses them anyway.
　　It's not the time now, Gramp,
to talk like it was the old days.   1020
It's the seventeenth century now;[12]
people live with more gusto. It's different.
　　If in your day people got married
at thirty or at forty,
we don't count that way today;   1025
life has speeded up.
　　Even little baby girls
before they have sense or reason
look up from their mother's breast
and say, "Daddy, I need a man."   1030
　　So the parents try to be modern:
they go and talk to the priest.
Too late. She says she's a woman;
she can pick a man for herself.
　　Gramp, I'm growing whiskers.   1035
And if I want to get married,
I have my reasons.

MELAMPO: 　　　　　　　　Which are?
DORISTO: Which are that I'm in love.
MELAMPO: Have you no shame?
DORISTO: 　　　　　　　　Well, no.
ARSINDO: 　　Oh, is it so awful, Melampo,   1040
to marry for love?
DORISTO: 　　　　　　　　My father
fell in love, too, once upon a time.
　　By God, Arsindo, since heaven
has made things come out as they are,
I have to get married today   1045
no matter how it upsets my Gramp.
ARSINDO: 　　Melampo, don't be unreasonable.
So the boy has taken a fancy
to get married.
MELAMPO: 　　　　　　　Is there anything worse?
ARSINDO: What harm can there be in that?   1050
MELAMPO: 　　What harm besides the fact
that his house will be utter chaos?
Something worse. I fear to think
of this babe at his tender age. . . .
　　He will incur offense
with his bride. You talk to him.

ARSINDO: Look, Doristo, for heaven's sake,   1055
            it's your own good he's thinking about.
                He wants you to marry someday.
            But right now you're just a lad,
            and your father is a little worried
            that your failure will shame us all.   1060
DORISTO: What failure?
ARSINDO: Your not being man enough
            yet to fulfill a wife.
DORISTO: He's afraid of that?
ARSINDO: So he's angry.
DORISTO: Better shock you now than later.
            Even though she's your daughter, Arsindo,   1065
            by God, I have to say it.
ARSINDO: I wish to heaven, Melampo,
            you'd just let him go in peace.
DORISTO: My house may not run very well —
            I won't argue that with you —   1070
            but as for fulfilling, I assure you. . . .
ARSINDO: What?
DORISTO: She's already pregnant.
ARSINDO: Pregnant?
DORISTO: Well, what do you want?
            I'm sorry; I couldn't help it.
ARSINDO: Why not?
MELAMPO: This is cock and bull.   1075
            She's lying so you'll marry her.
DORISTO: What do you mean she's lying?
            If you were in her condition,
            Gramp, they'd come all the way
            from Rome to see you, by God!   1080
ARSINDO: Melampo, a joke like this
            is not at all funny. Bartola
            is my daughter, my one and only.
            Is this sort of betrayal right?
MELAMPO: Tell me, boy, is it true?   1085
DORISTO: Gramp, I really don't know.
            One night I ran into her
            on the road to town, you know?
                And I pushed her into the bushes,
            not on purpose, just fooling around.   1090
            And she says she's having a baby.
            And now everybody's mad.

MELAMPO: She's having a baby? I'll kill her!

DORISTO: The devil take both of you.
Now they won't let me get married   1095
because I'm *not* too young.
    If I did wrong and did it right,
what is the punishment for?

ARSINDO: Melampo, if you are my friend,
you must see honour satisfied   1100
by whatever means there is.

MELAMPO: All right. I wash my hands.
Go tell them to fetch the priest
and bring him to the house.

[Enter Antonio and the Duchess
dressed as peasants]

ARSINDO: I'll go myself.

[Exit Arsindo]

ANTONIO: Look,   1105
here are two peasants, madam.
It's all the better, I think,
they are not shepherds of mine.

DUCHESS: Is this the right way to the village?

MELAMPO: This good man is headed that way.   1110

DORISTO: He's going to fetch the priest.

ANTONIO: For a happy reason, I hope.
    If not, I am sorry.

MELAMPO: For a happy.

ANTONIO: Well then, congratulations.
And when he comes, I hope   1115
you congratulate me, too.
    When will he be here?

MELAMPO: In an hour.

ANTONIO: I have a still better plan.

DUCHESS: What is it?

ANTONIO: The priest they have sent for
will pass this way in an hour.
    I will lie down by the road;   1120
you will tell him I am dying
of a wound, and say to him
that I am not your husband,
    and I fear for my salvation.
Pray him to marry us   1125
so that if I should die
the good Lord may pardon me.

	In the face of a present danger,	
	he will forgo the banns	
	and marry us on the spot.	1130
	And married, we may go home.	
DUCHESS:	A pretty mountain scheme.	
ANTONIO:	Come; we'll intercept him.	

[*Exit Antonio and the Duchess*]

DORISTO:	Who will be the best man?	
MELAMPO:	Go put your new suit on.	1135
	Your uncle will have to do it.	
DORISTO:	Well then, I'd better fetch him.	
	The house is a ways from here	
	and I don't know if he's home.	
	You know his master, the steward	1140
	of Her Excellency the Duchess,	
	sent for him yesterday in a hurry.	
MELAMPO:	Go, go.	
DORISTO:	I'm on my way.	
MELAMPO:	Pray heaven he's at home	1145
	and that he can bring your aunt.	
DORISTO:	[*Aside*]	
	O pardon, *Barlola mía*,	
	that I said what I said that you were.	

ACT II

[*Enter Ottavio de Medici, Servants,*
and Urbino, the secretary]

(3) OTTAVIO: Are you sure you told the Duchess
they were letters from her brother?

URBINO: She cares nothing for brothers now.
Her tyrannous illness rules.

OTTAVIO: I am grieved to hear she is ill.   5
    For two years I have been forced
to be away in Rome;
yet my love has only increased,
as if the pain of absence
only served to redouble its strength.   10
    And now that my affairs are settled
I have sued to Julio, her brother,
in regard to my marrying her,
and he has replied most warmly
that he consents if the lady will.   15
    But since he knows her intention
to flee any thought of marriage,
he has, mindful of my affection,
written letters to her himself
to see if he might move her.   20
    I should like very much to deliver them
in person.

URBINO: It has been two months now
she has been living like this.

OTTAVIO: I wish you would tell her, Urbino,
that she ought to consider my love,   25
    and my blood, and who I am.
When her own flesh and blood intercedes
how can she not be moved?
And if flesh and blood will not move her,

yet love must move flesh and blood.   30
    Is she being quite candid, Urbino?
Is she by any chance
feigning illness to avoid my suit?
Is it my sorry lot
to have closed the portals of her pity?   35
    For two months now, you say,
she's been abed. It almost
seems as though my coming,
and the knowledge of my deathless passion,
make her sick. What say you, hey?   40
    Tell me the truth, Urbino.
Is it because of me
that this illness has overcome her?
For there's nothing like an unwanted suitor
to bring plague upon a house.   45
    Did she instruct you to tell me
she was ill?

URBINO: Alas, Ottavio,
I'm surprised that you had not heard.
It's true. There's no doubt of it.
She's been sick these two months in her bed.   50
You may not see her today,
but I'll take the letters to her,
and if she improves tomorrow
I will have Livia ask
if you may have an audience.   55

OTTAVIO: Having kept her health for two years
while I was away in Rome,
she now decides to be ill!

URBINO: No, this has happened before;
it is not the first time, Ottavio.   60
    Last year at about this time
she suffered a similar illness.

OTTAVIO: Then she was ill once before
just after I left for Rome.

URBINO: Almost to the point of death.   65
It is all melancholic humour.

OTTAVIO: She is young, and she is a widow.
Do you have her ear?

URBINO: Not lately.
And I have certain reasons
to think I should leave her service.   70

I am not alone in her confidence.
Indeed, I am so far forgotten
that I scarcely put pen to paper.
Antonio, her steward, is the one
that governs her estate.   75
    She lives through him: he disposes.
He gives, takes away, makes the law.

OTTAVIO: A good man?
URBINO: · A very good man.
OTTAVIO: He served the kings of France
in Naples.
URBINO: No one questions   80
his advancement. But I fear he wrongs me
in courting a certain lady
whom I hope to marry myself.
OTTAVIO: Is that Livia?
URBINO: Her name is Livia[13]
But she does not alleviate my pain.   85

[Enter Antonio]

ANTONIO: My lady the Duchess (who is
in most extreme distress
that she cannot speak with you,
for the illness leaves her no peace
and will not abate for a moment)   90
assures you, my lord Ottavio,
that she will inform you as soon
as heaven gives her ease
when, decently attired,
she may see you.
OTTAVIO: Well then, very well.   95
From the depths of my misfortune
I assumed that she feigned this pass.
But now that I see it is real,
I would have you tell your lady
I am sensible of her illness,   100
    and give myself only the license
to send her a few small gifts
while I remain in Amalfi.
Tell her I shall wait upon her
when she can rise to receive me.   105
    For, having maintained such decorum,
I imagine that she would scruple
to receive me in her bed.

ANTONIO: Indeed. You know already
             how scrupulous she is.   110
             As chaste as Zenobia.[14]
OTTAVIO: Well, gentlemen, fare you well.
                                              [*Exit Ottavio*]
ANTONIO: God save you, Urbino.
URBINO: Nay,
             rather than he should save me,
             let him save our friendship, Antonio.   115
                 Now that Ottavio is gone,
             you must hear what just complaints
             I have of your strange behaviour.
ANTONIO: Love is a certain deceiver,
             the dream of a wandering mind.   120
                 Have you never seen, Urbino,
             on the blue veil of the sky,
             some clouds, that we give names to?
             Sometimes we call them serpents,
             or ships, or men, or cattle?
                 Well, a lover's imagination
             paints such clouds upon itself:
             called "suspicion" or "betrayal."
             But eventually they dissolve,
             being only clouds of the mind.
                 Open your eyes, Urbino,
             and see that I do not offend you.
URBINO: This is crocodile concern:
             weeping piteous tears
             while you work to destroy my life![15]   135
                 I finally summoned the courage
             (much to my sorrow now)
             to beseech the Duchess to grant me
             Livia's hand in marriage,
             the prize I have sought for so long.   140
                 But the Duchess replied that Livia
             was already promised to you.
             If this be so, Antonio,
             are you a friend, or a hypocrite
             to deny your intentions to me?   145
                 Is this the promise you made me
             so many times over?
ANTONIO: I gave her
             no cause for this. I never

	sued to the Duchess for Livia.	
	Her Excellency only means	150
	to reward me with this marriage.	
	Since I am not in love with Livia,	
	why must she marry me off?	
	If she means to grant me a boon,	
	good God, what a burden she's made of it!	155
	I assure you upon my life	
	that I will not marry Livia.	
URBINO:	She will be offended.	
ANTONIO:	Well, it's useless for her to complain	
	if I fail to sue for her.	160
	And if it pains her to think	
	she is forced to marry me,	
	she may complain to the Duchess.	
URBINO:	Then you think, Antonio, my friend,	
	that my suit may fare well after all?	165
ANTONIO:	Be assured of it.	
URBINO:	Well then, I go	
	to plead my cause with the Duchess.	

[Exit Urbino]

ANTONIO:	Urbino, I am your friend.	
	Why should I not be? Alas,	
	what danger I find myself in!	170
	For two years now, secretly,	
	I have been married to the Duchess,	
	and I live in so happy a state,	
	so secure, so sweetly content,	
	that I might be the envy	175
	of any man in the world!	
	She gave me a son, who is raised	
	in such absolute secrecy	
	that a mountain is made the fortress	
	for this boy, who is my hope.	180
	And now her illness is feigned	
	for the birth of a daughter, so beautiful,	
	unless my love deceive me,	
	that Troy and Spain might both	
	be lost again for her.	185
	They are without question such	
	that even Latona's children	
	could not surpass these two.	
	For the same light crowns them also:	

one the sun, the other the moon.   190
O what children, blessed heaven!
O what glory! O what gifts!
Come night, obscure the earth.
If I call her my little moon,
you must keep her veiled for me.   195
    Moon of night my girl must be
when I bear her light away.
Come, Night. Be not afraid.
She cannot blaze out your shadows,
for I must wrap her up,   200
    and cover her with my cloak
to hide her splendour. Come.
I must go up into the hills.
Hide, Latona's daughter;
another moon comes out.   205
    Sun, you need not rise;
my son lights both day and night.
Alas, forgive me. Don't strike.
I am a father, and for love
I may say foolish things.   210
        [Exit Antonio; Enter Urbino by night]

URBINO: The Duchess' plans have put me
into torments of jealousy.
Even though they distress Antonio
— or he says that they distress him —
    I come here in the dead of night   215
to find out the truth myself:
to see if what he told me
reflects his real desires.
    He swore it was not his doing,
but incredulous jealousy   220
knows that an amorous passion
will betray the truest friend.
    Here Livia spoke with me
when I lived in her good grace.
Here she told me that she loved me,   225
and I told her my love in turn.
    If Antonio in secret pursues
that marriage the Duchess proposed,
and if, in effect, his tongue
contradicts his heart in this,   230
    he will certainly have recourse

to this selfsame place to woo her.
This denial he makes to me
is only a clever ruse,
     and he will make the excuse   235
that the Duchess forces it on him.
But I am the one who, thereafter,
will pay the price for him.
     Then I must perforce impede it
or at least prove for myself   240
if a sword can wound as deeply
as the tongue of a hypocrite.
     God save me! Who is it that opened
that secret door in the wall?
Ah well, for the man of the house   245
it will always be ajar!
     It leads to a little staircase
that winds up to the Duchess' chamber.
Disillusion, with what dispatch
you snatch the mists away!   250

                                 [Enter Livia with an infant
                                         in her arms]

LIVIA: Antonio!
URBINO: She calls Antonio,
and that voice is Livia's voice!
Now will Antonio tell me,
"The Duchess forced me to!"
     Can I ask more grounds than this   255
for my jealousy and suspicion?
O night, O stars, O heaven,
bear witness how I am deceived!
LIVIA: Antonio!
URBINO: Why hold back?
I'll pretend I am Antonio.   260
I am in so fierce a passion
that I fear what will come of it.
     Here I am.
LIVIA: Then take her quickly.
I cannot linger here.
Good night.

                                        [Exit Livia after
                            giving Urbino the child]
URBINO: Like a man asleep,   265
I have formed this chimera[16] dreaming.

Blessed heaven! Have I my senses?
What is this she's given me?
The thing is living; it cried!
Did it cry? I think it did.   270
      No doubt. It is a baby.
A bitter fate is mine —
or its — for on this day
it is born into hell.
      If it was my intention   275
to lay my fears to rest,
by God they are resting now.
This is proof enough for me.
      I had not looked for this,
only for a man speaking softly,   280
not a child, a crying child,
crying the lie out loud.
      Other men are told their folly
in words, but I have here
the fruits of labour, works   285
to work my disenchantment.
      What is there left to know?
What proofs shall I require?
This living, breathing proof
will suffice me. It is enough.   290
      Torments of jealousy,
what more do you seek than this?
Behold, a revelation
with hands and eyes and feet!
      They say that love and suspicion   295
are the parents of jealousy.
Then the heavens have joined these two
to give me the childbed pain.
      So close an intimacy,
so blatant the fruit of it!   300
This creature has been born
of their love and my suspicion.
      Many have longed to see
this thing we call jealousy,
so vague, so elusive, so various,   305
so hard to comprehend.
      Some say it is spectacles,
that make little things seem large;
some say a prismatic stone

that tricks a lover's eye.   310
    Some say it is envy, and some
say trust that was had and lost,
and some say it's a monster
that's bred out of fear and rumour.
    But I, after much long watching,   315
I say they may all come and see,
anyone who would see it living:
this child is jealousy.
    A man is coming. Doubtless
it is Antonio.

                           [Enter Antonio by night]

ANTONIO: Am I late?   320
Someone has kept me who turns
my rejoicing into grief.
    Ottavio has come again
to sue for marriage to the Duchess. . . .
Hush, there is someone here.   325
My God! Who can it be?
    He has seen me. Then it were well
that I find out who it is.
Can it be Ottavio followed me
after I spoke to him?   330
    Heaven help me. I've never seen
anyone here at night,
not even passing by.
Everything conspires against me.
    I don't know what I dreamed last night: 335
but today Ottavio came,
and Urbino challenged me.
He is waiting. What shall I do?
    Well, there's no help for it.
Hah, sirrah! Do you not think, sir,   340
that you offend this house
to come here and loiter about?
    Are you not aware
that the Duchess is sequestered?
I spied you from the balcony   345
and with no small concern
    I came down to put you out.
Be gone, sir. I am the chief steward.

URBINO: Chief steward? You are the chief traitor!
You have betrayed me, Antonio.   350

ANTONIO: Is that Urbino?

URBINO: Is that
what your word is worth?

ANTONIO: I have not
broken my word to you.
I do not deserve this rebuke.

URBINO: You deserve a rebuke from my sword   355
for a base and treacherous villain!
But my hands are only too full
of blood of yours already.
    Though I think it would not be amiss
if I made a buckler of it,   360
and then let your own sword
avenge me even better.
    When I came here, Livia called me
— she mistook me for you, of course —
and she lingered just long enough   365
to give me what you see here.
    How is it, Antonio, that you
get children of Livia, while claiming
she is forced on you? A fine pretense.
What an excellent steward you make!   370
    You enjoy her with so much license
that you breed on her, and yet
it grieves you the Duchess should marry you.
Kisses and embraces
are called "palace fruit" sometimes,   375
but this dish, no, not this.
The man that comes this far
has partaken of more than is honest.
    There, take up your child, Antonio.
Never say we were two against you.   380
The child is another you,
and I suffer in touching it.
    Bear it away from harm;
it is your obligation.
I shall take satisfaction later   385
for your treachery to me.
    For its innocence' sake I hold off,
though I feel myself a bawd,
if not to your match, yet still
to the shame of this bastardy.   390
    O, you give good account

of our lady the Duchess' honour!
By heaven, I am sorry now
to have given the child to you.
  You don't deserve it, nay,   395
it had been more loyal of me
to have shown Her Excellency
this unimpeachable witness.
  So tender in years and yet
I think it would be believed.   400
Little thing, as light as it is
it would prove your levity.
  But enough. I will tell the Duchess
how her treacherous chief steward,
being my chief cause of sorrow   405
has contrived her chief dishonour.

           [*Exit Urbino*]

(4) ANTONIO: Was ever a man so confounded as this?
How should it happen to anyone
that after two years, just one day's error
should publish a love that has been so secret? 410
But I have no right to bemoan this chance;
fortune is mercifully cruel to me:
after all that has happened today, the worst
has missed the mark at which it was aimed.
  Urbino is deceived by his passion for Livia.
Jealousy has done me some good turn. 416
There's haven in this, by heaven; I owe him
a debt for his doubts. They may save us yet.
He is blind from watching so anxiously,
and when he is handed Camila's honour, 420
he mistakes it for Livia's; as things stand,
it is she who now suffers the shame of it.
  Whatever he may tell the Duchess
the fury will not redound up on me.
And his vengeance can therefore do no harm 425
that I cannot find some means to repair.
My soul's little girl, ride swiftly now.
Misfortunes would make an end to me,
and if they see to whom you are sent,
they will know I am their man.   430
  Angel, book of all my secrets,
I must guard you lest anyone read, for here
love's deepest mystery is writ

with secret signs, not to be known.
I am a steward, and you my ledger;   435
let no eye study my accounts.
Since I am humble and my mistress great,
our gettings might get us bankruptcy.
   Come, sweetheart, and join your lusty brother
with those honest peasants up on the mountain
who with their plain and trusty hearts   441
will nurture you and love you well.
Let heaven with a merciful hand protect
your innocence for greater things
to come. And that which heaven defends   445
man shall be powerless to harm.
                    [*They exit; enter Doristo and Bartola, peasants*]

(3) DORISTO: I have to go to town
                 no matter how much you cry.

BARTOLA: Ah, now you show what you are!

DORISTO: Who can put up with this?   450
                    Did I marry you, Bartola,
                 to be always and forever with you?

BARTOLA: At least. And God commands
                 that you love me, and me alone.

DORISTO: Who told you that?

BARTOLA: Oh lovely!   455
                 The priest that married me.

DORISTO: Well, don't I comply with that?
                 The whole mountain knows I do.

BARTOLA: No, you don't. You go away,
                 and I'm eaten with jealousy.   460

DORISTO: You've no cause to complain of me.

BARTOLA: Oh, Doristo, I can't help it.

DORISTO: This jealousy, Bartola,
                 belongs in the city, not here.

BARTOLA: Well then, don't make me jealous   465
                 if you think it belongs in the city.
                    But blessed heaven knows
                 that anywhere there's love
                 there's jealousy, Doristo,
                 and it makes people miserable.   470
                    It would be like the clock in the village
                 without any wheels inside,
                 like a hook without any onions,

or the cupboard without any dishes,
    like a house that has no ceiling   475
and a garden without a gardener,
like a mortar without a pestle,
like a stove without a fire,
    like baptism without water,
or an ugly tart without rouge,   480
like a frying pan without oil
and a distaff without fleece,
    like crumbs without bacon fat,
like a sick man with no afflictions,
like a drum with no drumsticks,   485
like a pack without an ass,
    like a cabbage with no leaves
or a farm with no farmhouse,
like a husband and wife with no children:
that's love without jealousy.   490

DORISTO: You are very wise, Bartola.
It makes my hair stand on end
to see how clever you are.
Where can you have been studying?
    Have you found some book of the priest's?
When were you in his study?   496

BARTOLA: Love teaches me, Doristo,
and purges me in its fire.

DORISTO: Love? I'll wager the sacristan
has been giving you some lessons.   500

BARTOLA: The art of the heart is taught
in the schoolroom of suffering.

DORISTO: Good God!

BARTOLA: But tell me now,
aren't we all schooled by love?

DORISTO: Bartola, just let me go.   505
You have to just let me go.
    It isn't wise for a woman
to hold her husband captive.
Let me live free and happy;
I'm not going to sully our vows.   510
    If I'm to be always at home
and always looking at you,
you have to realize
what you see all the time gets ugly.
    A woman that day after day   515

you see the same way in the same house
looks like a chair, not a woman.
Like a board you knead your bread on.
    She looks more like a ladle rack
than a woman. And so it's only right   520
that a man's taste be whetted a bit,
that a husband go out a little.
    Besides, a man discovers
little things that get on his nerves
when he's with someone every minute;   525
little things you can't put a name to.
    You watch her screw up her hair,
with the little jars and the mirror,
and a woman that's only sketched in
is a terrible thing to see.   530
    But to come when she's all fixed up
and the table is set — now that
is agreeable, neat, and clean.
It's the process I don't want to see.
    The gift of a woman's presence   535
must be something like a pie:
Just serve it to me when it's done,
and spare me the mess while you make it.
    Whether they're single or married,
women are plagued by one fancy: 540
when they're single, that they need entreating;
when they're married, that they must entreat.
    I think some people are coming.

BARTOLA: It's only one man. He's dismounted
and is tying his horse.

DORISTO: Here he comes.   545

[Enter Antonio]

ANTONIO: I have ridden to outstrip the wind,
    but the day has come faster yet:
it has caught up with me.
But at least by the time the dawn reached me
I was well out of anyone's sight.   550
    There are two peasants standing
by the garden wall. Good morning!
Which farmhouse is Bartola's?

BARTOLA: He must have lost his way.

DORISTO: But just now he said your name.   555

BARTOLA: Isn't that the master?

DORISTO:	It is.
BARTOLA:	Let us kiss your feet, my lord.
ANTONIO:	Is that Doristo?
DORISTO:	Of course.
ANTONIO:	And Bartola?
BARTOLA:	Can't you see?
ANTONIO:	How's my son?
DORISTO:	He's grown two whiskers.

560

BARTOLA: Well. By first threshing time
he'll be putting his foot on the harrow.

ANTONIO: Is your baby born?

BARTOLA: Alas,
six days ago we buried him.

DORISTO: Either I am cursed   565
or it was fortold for us.
    Everyone said to me
that the boy should go into the Church.
They said if we gave to the Church,
the Church would some day give to us.   570
    Well, we gave him up so promptly
that without any vows or orders
he's theirs till Judgment Day.

ANTONIO: How fortunate I have been!

BARTOLA: If anyone needs a wet nurse,   575
you know how I nurse my babies.
You know that yours (which is mine)
weaned now a year and a half,
    is like an elephant.
Just you send him to me.   580

ANTONIO: I know of one that needs you,
and I have her here, Bartola.
    This is my fair little girl,
sister to the other boy.
Such a sun needs a young companion,   585
a little dawn, a star.

BARTOLA: Give her to me. Ah, bless her,
what a lovely face, my lord.
Who could have hoped for this!

DORISTO: Give her a charm,[17] Bartola.   590

BARTOLA: Yes, a thousand. God keep thee!
What a giggle! She's talking to me!

ANTONIO: It bodes well. I was lucky
to have found the two of you.

BARTOLA: By heaven and my grandfather's nose,   595
I know what she's saying, yes:
she wants to nurse. Look what light
shines out of those bright little eyes!
　　Yes, baby, sweetheart, my life.
My little duchess.
ANTONIO: 　　　　　　All is well.   600
DORISTO: Now what do you make of this?
You see? She's now stark raving mad.
　　The baby's been talking two days
and requests a pull at the breast.
Even the soberest woman   605
goes ga-ga at baby prattle.
If the baby so much as coughs
her mama swears she said, "Daddy."
ANTONIO: Let's go see my son.
And let me leave you some money   610
while I'm here, my good foster-parents.
DORISTO: Your horse?
ANTONIO: 　　　　　　He's tied over there.
DORISTO: We can see him from the house;
there are always herders about.
Did you take the bit out?
ANTONIO: 　　　　　　　　No.
But he seems to be grazing with it.
BARTOLA: All lilies and carnations!
This is the baby I bore.
　　It is living; I'm comforted.
Go where you will, Doristo.   620
DORISTO: Will you truly let me go?
BARTOLA: I have this darling to amuse me.
DORISTO: 　　Don't you love me any more?
BARTOLA: Never mind my loving you.
This blessed little girl   625
is the one I love the most.
DORISTO: Well, if that's how you comfort yourself,
I can do the same thing myself.
I'll find me a girl to take care of
— a little girl about fifteen.   630
　　　　　[*They exit; the Duchess and Urbino enter*]
(4-3) DUCHESS: If this confidence comes from Ottavio again
I've no wish to hear it, Urbino.
URBINO: It is not from Ottavio, Excellency.

	I think you make sport of him,	
	and indeed of all the suitors that court you.	635
DUCHESS:	Then what can you have to confide?	
URBINO:	After such a long, melancholic seige,	
	that kept you abed for two months,	
	when your ladyship finally rises up	
	to gladden all her estate,	640
	and everyone, vassal and servant, rejoices,	
	I am loathe to repay that joy	
	with matter that may grieve Your Excellency.	
DUCHESS:	Is it something unpleasant, then,	
	that you have to confide?	
URBINO:	Perhaps your wit	645
	may turn it to better purpose.	
	Thus an ancient wise man painted wit	
	holding a balance in her hand.	
	On one scale lay all the spoils of chance:	
	wrecked ships and lost advantage,	650
	with lofty honours tumbled down	
	and hard-got sceptres and empires,	
	the laurels, the triumphs, the feats of arms . . .	
	on the other, a single feather.	
DUCHESS:	I am not in the mood to have you vex me.	655
URBINO:	You mistake me.	
DUCHESS:	Bless you, go.	
URBINO.	This is the way all women govern.	
	Pray heaven the day comes soon	
	when you may repent your scorn of me.	
DUCHESS:	Come back.	
URBINO:	I mean only your good.	660
DUCHESS:	We shall see. Well, what seems to you so dire?	
URBINO:	It is not "seems to me" that last night	
	as I happened to stroll by the terrace, Livia,	
	thinking I was Antonio, called,	
	and handed me proof of her infamy.	665
DUCHESS:	What proof?	
URBINO:	A newborn baby	
	wrapped in a mantle.	
DUCHESS:	Sweet God in heaven!	
	And you think?	
URBINO:	The child was hers.	
	And Antonio certainly fathered it.	
DUCHESS:	It was a baby?	

URBINO:	Yes. 670
	Antonio has come to Livia's bed.
DUCHESS:	Why, you were dreaming.
URBINO:	So.
	And therefore, like a dreaming man,
	I threw it into a ditch.
DUCHESS:	You demon! What did you say?
URBINO:	I said 675
	if it was a dream, does it matter?
DUCHESS:	Listen, in God's name, for if it's the truth
	it is pity I feel, not outrage.
URBINO:	Well then, it is true what I said of Livia,
	but I did not harm the child. 680
	Antonio came for it.
DUCHESS:	Then who has it?
URBINO:	I gave it to him.
DUCHESS:	Well done.
	We must look to a God above all things.
	I am greatly outraged, but still
	this is a soul that cost God his blood. 685
	Alas for the honour of my house!
	Antonio, to whom I trusted all,
	has he done such a thing? Call Livia.
URBINO:	My lady, if the household knows of this,
	it cannot be but soon 690
	all Italy will know, and then
	some evil minds will say
	(who are ignorant of you and of your virtue)
	things that may disgrace you.
DUCHESS:	What do you advise, secretary, my friend? 695
	Urbino, what shall I do?
	Sweet heaven! Shall I call my brothers?
URBINO:	Ah,
	but if you can mend it in secret,
	why risk such a public contingency?
DUCHESS:	Shall I put him to death?
URBINO:	That would be 700
	at least more prudent.
DUCHESS:	Antonio die!
	But what am I saying? I cannot
	without arousing suspicion. Nay,
	is he not a gentleman?
	It is better to marry them.

URBINO:	If you do, 705
	then some will suspect that you knew,
	and that you give countenance to such things.
DUCHESS:	Then what can I do?
URBINO:	Dismiss him.
DUCHESS:	Good, well said. And Livia shall not
	be told the reason for it. 710
	I'll expel the traitor from my house,
	and afterwards punish them fully.
	O prudent advice! O sapient Urbino!
	How little I've valued your wisdom!
	But now that heaven has chastened me 715
	it is you that shall govern my house.
	You shall be my right hand, my authority.
	Summon the servants, Urbino.
	And Antonio, too.
URBINO:	In this way, madam,
	you may handle it all discreetly. 720
	[Exit Urbino]
(5) DUCHESS:	How cruel an accident, my own Antonio!
	What could have detained you so disastrously?
	But still, as long as our deception holds
	it is foolish to say we are unfortunate.
	When my son was born, he might have
	published
	everything we had so long concealed. 726
	But there was secrecy and strictest care;
	a manly force accompanied his birth.
	When my daughter comes, the childbed joy
	she should bring with her changes names with woe;
	my honour is now anyone's opinion. 731
	Nay, daughter, 'tis not strange it's come to pass
	your father should be shadowed by your birth;
	when a woman's born, a man's ruin begins.
	[Enter Furio, Filelfo, Dinarco,
	Ruperto, Urbino, and Celso]
(3) URBINO:	Here are Furio and Ruperto, 735
	Filelfo and Dinarco also.
FURIO:	Madam?
DUCHESS:	Now certainly
	I set sail on a sea of dishonour,
	and death is the only port.
	Is Antonio not here?

FILELFO: Someone said   740
            he has just come back, my lady.

                                        [*Enter Antonio*]

ANTONIO: Has the Duchess called for me?
            My lady?
DUCHESS: I fall to pieces.
            I dissemble, while my soul weeps.
ANTONIO: What would Your Excellency?   745
            Why are so many servants gathered?
DUCHESS: My household is here to witness,
            because someone must be dismissed
            from my presence and from my employ.
                Furio, since you served the Duke   750
            (he that is now in heaven)
            and have been always loyal,
            in reward for your honest zeal
            I neither rebuke nor dismiss you.
                I know if my house goes poorly,   755
            well, it is a woman's house.
FURIO: All your chief servants are here.
            I think that some minor offense
            has received a tremendous report.[18]
                I have never seen such a thing   760
            as this proceeding, madam.
FILELFO: Some base, unworthy fellow
            that Your Excellency trusts
            has told you some fabrication
                that will prove to be nothing but windmills.
DUCHESS: It grieves me to say, Filelfo,   766
            it is only too well grounded.
            But I know you are wise and prudent;
            I'm aware of your good sense.
                You likewise may remain in my house.   770
            Like Furio, you have served me well.
FILELFO: You have well repaid me, madam.
DINARCO: I am abashed, my lady,
            to have everyone's eyes on me.
                Am I the one that offends you?   775
DUCHESS: No, Dinarco.
DINARCO: Because you know
            I have always been loyal to you.
CELSO: But how is evil to spring up

	where there's never a thought of it?	
	Can it possibly be these white hairs	780
	that have given you cause to complain?	
	Because early and late together	
	these portals and gates, look you,	
	these windows and corridors	
	all know that I have not shirked	785
	the littlest jot in fulfilling	
	my appointed obligations.	

DUCHESS: Celso, who could suggest
that you could anger me?
I respect you like a father.   790

CELSO: Well, now my tears speak for me
and show what tender intentions
I have, good madam.

RUPERTO: Now
you will let the secret out.
Can it be Ruperto?   795

DUCHESS: No, not you.

URBINO: Then it must be I.
For it certainly is not Antonio.
It cannot have been he
that has incurred your displeasure.

DUCHESS: Not Ruperto, and not Urbino.   800

ANTONIO: Then it is I? No answer.
Already I imagine the cause.
And you hide your face from me;
then someone has played the informer.
But you cannot condemn a man   805
to whom you have trusted your house,
your property, honour, your son,
without at least hearing him.
Oh, they have done their work well.
I will not reply to it then.   810
I know you have reasons enough.
But whoever it was that so promptly
came up to inform on me
shall promptly be weeping for it.

DUCHESS: O, you impudent villain!   815
A dishonour to this house!
No, spare me your bold reply;
I know everything that has passed.
Loyalty and justice prevail.

	Leave my house at once.	820
CELSO:	[To Furio]	
	What can the steward have done	
	that she pitches him out like this?	
FURIO:	I don't know.	
DUCHESS:	If I refrain	
	from punishing you and her,	
	it is because I know	825

                             [*She approaches and stands near him*]

	[*Softly to him*]	
	Oh, Antonio, I must feign all this	
	because he saw and he knows.	
ANTONIO:	[*Softly to her*]	
	Prudently done, my lady,	
	under the circumstances.	
DUCHESS:	[*Aloud*]	
	Leave my house at once.	830
	[*Aside to him*]	
	My glory, my life, my husband,	
	all my joy departs with you;	
	in such a tearful exile	
	my heart will wither and die.	
	[*Aloud*]	
	If you linger a single moment	835
	you'll be put to death.	
ANTONIO:	Yet heaven	
	will vindicate me, madam.	
	[*Softly*]	
	With what strange uneasiness	
	do I part from thee, my darling.	
DUCHESS:	[*Softly*]	
	Don't be uneasy, love.	840
	You shall see me secretly.	
ANTONIO:	[*Aloud*]	
	While you are angry, madam,	
	I can say no more to you	
	[*Softly*]	
	than that I love you, Camila,	
	and I carried our daughter away.	845
	And, as luck would have it,	
	the woman who nursed our boy	
	gave birth six days ago	
	but today I found her childless.	

DUCHESS: [*Aloud*]
           There is no excuse. Get out.   850
           [*Softly*]
           Then is her baby dead?

ANTONIO: [*Softly*]
           Her grief was swept away
           with the new nursling in her arms.

DUCHESS: [*Softly*]
           God save both nurse and child.
           And save us, in spite of my brothers.   855
           You shall be mine. Hush now!

ANTONIO: [*Aloud*]
           How can you dishonour me
           on a villain's word. Is this
           what I have deserved at your hands?

DUCHESS: Filelfo, take his accounts.   860
           Come with me, Urbino.
           Do not speak any more of this outrage
           or I'll have your life.

ANTONIO: Not a word.
           I say nothing. But I feel much.

DUCHESS: Then may you find refuge in it.   865
                        [*Exit the Duchess*]

URBINO: He has got what he deserves.
           And without him I get the honour.
            Why should I keep his secrets
            when I've been deceived by him?
                What's more, as for loyalty   870
           I owe it more to the Duchess
            than a man who's disloyal to me.
                          [*Exit Urbino*]

FURIO: Antonio, I'm very sorry
           that a man of your reputation
                has given Her Excellency   875
           such occasion for displeasure.

ANTONIO: They are all false accusations.

FILELFO: Be prudent here, Antonio.
           Exercise discretion.
                I know nothing of your guilt or innocence.
           It may be a passing fury.   881

DINARCO: By God, I'm deeply sorry
                for this fury then, Antonio.
           And I'm furious at Urbino;

He envies you.

ANTONIO: So much   885
that he has done this to me.

CELSO: I have never seen such a villain.
Whatever honours you earned,
he has suffered with very bad grace.
                But it's only a woman's humour.   890
Give her a day or two.

ANTONIO: Celso, we cannot pretend
that some childish little thing
could undo me, as I am a man.
                All of you know that I served   895
with her uncle, the King of Naples,
that he held me in high estimation
and never had cause to use me
as you see here I have been used.
                Ah, the power of princes   900
to make and unmake a man!

CELSO: We shall all go in fear from now on.

ANTONIO: And my honour, too, from now on
must walk in the shadow of this.

                            [*They exit; enter Ottavio and*
                            Fabricio prepared to go hunting]

OTTAVIO: Then have that Spanish stallion   905
saddled and ready for me.

FABRICIO: He is fine enough to be
the sun's own steed, my lord.
                What appointments shall I put on?

OTTAVIO: The scarlet and silver ones.   910

FABRICIO: A lovesick hunter's colours.
They'll have reason to call you that.
                Green is correct for the field.

OTTAVIO: Green does not suit me, Fabricio.
While I live without fresh hope   915
how can I ride out in green?
                The Duchess disprizes me
when I've served her now three years.

FABRICIO: And with such a weight of rebuffs
you still pursue this suit?   920

OTTAVIO: What can I do, Fabricio,
if I was born to love her,
this celestial woman,
this angel of my reason,

	this Circe of my illusion,	925
	this moon of my blood's tide,	
	where I, beseeching favour,	
	receive only endless rebuke?	
	I ride out into the woods	
	to scatter my brooding thoughts	930
	and to let the wind dispel	
	the last of my treacherous hopes.	
	Pray God the forest keeps thee	
	and thou dost not return with me!	
	O hope, expire on my sighs	935
	and let me rest in peace.	
FABRICIO:	As for giving up hope	
	when a man is in love, let a prudent man	
	or prudent enough, you know,	
	offer this pungent conceit.	940
	There are certain harpoons, my lord,	
	that are fastened to the arm by a cord,	
	and return more the forcefully	
	the harder you fling them away.[19]	
	So with a man in love	945
	when hope has been cast off:	
	sometimes the torments depart	
	to return with still greater fury.	
OTTAVIO:	A telling analogy,	
	for the more I thrust them away,	950
	the more fiercely they strike again	
	at my already languishing breast.	
	[Enter Urbino]	
URBINO:	Ottavio rides out today.	
OTTAVIO:	O, secretary!	
URBINO:	My lord,	
	what is this?	
OTTAVIO:	The follies of love	955
	and a wise man's remedy:	
	They advise one to exercise.	
	I am going to hunt with Fabricio.	
URBINO:	It's a good thing, exercise;	
	it eases the mind a good deal.	960
OTTAVIO:	What news of that cruel angel?	
URBINO:	She is extremely wroth	
	and has retired with it.	
OTTAVIO:	Retired with her wrath, is she?	

O God, would I were that wrath!   965
May we know the reason for it?

URBINO: The reasons are household matters.
Any shadow will set her off.

OTTAVIO: I have the most dire suspicions.
Is it I?

URBINO: You, my lord? Why you?   970
She is angry with her steward.

OTTAVIO: Jesu! With her steward?
    I should think it less impossible
for Spain to nurture lions,
or fire to breed chameleons,   975
or air bright salamanders,
    for lemons to grow in Scythia,
or snow fall on Ethiops.[20]

URBINO: It happens that she herself
has called him to account,   980
    and taking him aside,
she has dealt so roundly with him
that neither his wit could save him
nor delaying neither, by God!
    The steward has been dismissed.   985

OTTAVIO: Dismissed? This is grave indeed.
And no one knows the reason?

URBINO: I suspect the reason is known
    but cannot be talked about.

OTTAVIO: Why not? By God, Urbino,   990
it will kill me not to know.

URBINO: Well, you must die then, my lord.
    By the faith of a gentleman,
I cannot reveal it to you.

OTTAVIO: I marvel that I am who I am   995
and you value me so little!
    Fabricio, stand apart.

FABRICIO: I'll wait outside.

OTTAVIO: Now, Urbino,
I'm alone.

URBINO: It's a shameful case.

OTTAVIO: You will drive me mad, Urbino.   1000

URBINO: You must give me your word of honour
as a gentleman, Ottavio,
to keep silent, for it is a disgrace
that may touch on more than one.

	And because out of my affection	1005
	and friendship for you I tell you,	
	is no reason	
OTTAVIO:	Urbino, my friend,	
	you needn't finish the reason.	
	By the living God I swear	
	I shall never tell a soul!	1010
URBINO:	Last night, it having struck one,	
	I was roused by some accident	
	to walk out upon the terrace.	
	Livia emerged from a doorway	
	and called out, "Antonio, Antonio!"	1015
	I approached, about to speak,	
	when she thrust (I tremble to say it)	
	a baby into my arms.	
	I would rather have taken a flogging	
	or a knife against my throat!	1020
	In short, she believed she gave it	
	to her own Antonio, since he	
	came up at the very moment	
	when I clasped it in my arms.	
	I gave it to him, and I flung	1025
	his betrayal in his face.	
	My loyalty is to this house	
	as befits a gentleman,	
	and I informed the Duchess,	
	just up from her sickbed today.	1030
OTTAVIO:	But who did you think bore the child?	
URBINO:	Livia.	
OTTAVIO:	What a wit is that?	
	Are you such a fool?	
URBINO:	Then who?	
OTTAVIO:	These two months sick in bed	
	were to cover her pregnancy;	1035
	that seems a more likely answer.	
	And by my life, Urbino,	
	and by the Duke, my lord,	
	the Duchess of Amalfi	
	has a secret lover.	
URBINO:	No,	1040
	I cannot imagine anyone . . .	
	and in the house; it is nonsense.	
	Today I barely prevented	

her putting Antonio to death.
    And you know how sequestered she is.   1045

OTTAVIO: Don't be fooled by hypocrisies.

URBINO: But my jealous fantasies
have at least some sound foundation.
    The Duchess has dismissed Antonio,
and taken his accounts,   1050
and this in public disgrace.
And she wept and hid herself.
    By all this, it's not Antonio.

OTTAVIO: You know little of widow's weeds.
The nets of the devil himself   1055
are not such a subtle web.
    The Duchess has born a child
as I am myself.

URBINO: But by whom?

OTTAVIO: By a ghostly incubus
unseen by those he oppresses.   1060
    I have been amazed before now
to see such youth in mourning,
for a woman is not a field
that bears fruit without husbandry.

URBINO: By God, I should rejoice   1065
although infamy falls on her.
But still, my lord, consider . . . .

OTTAVIO: Nothing. The guilt is clear.

URBINO: But how could she trust Antonio
with her honour, and then dismiss him?   1070

OTTAVIO: What better testimony
to the truth of my suspicions?
    Don't you see that to cover her guilt
she pretends to cast him off?
And this huddling with the accounts —   1075
do you think they did it to quarrel?
    Send word to her brothers at once.
As a gentleman.

URBINO: My lord,
We had better weigh this first,
and examine these suppositions.   1080
    When they're proven, I myself
will be the first to fell him
though he flee to the heart of hell.

OTTAVIO: And me, what shall I do?   1085

Alas, I shall lose my mind.
Urbino, Camila is wicked.
A common Jezebel.[21]

URBINO: Where are you going?
OTTAVIO: To tell
my grief to the wilderness.
I shall die; I am bursting apart!   1090
Was dying of love not enough?
Must I die now of shame and rage?
        Heaven, curse your cruelty
the day she first came to my thoughts,
the day that I first beheld her,   1095
and beholding her, fell in love.
        O hills, I had meant to carry
my confusion into your fastnesses.
Now I bring my certain outrage.
Now I bring you the end of my days!   1100
        O, one of you topple down
upon my body. Or
let me topple from my horse.
Bear me lifeless to Camila!

                              [*Exit Ottavio*]

(5) URBINO: They used to say there was a king made war
in Africa, and then came home quite safe.   1106
I've heard of lightning menacing a branch
and yet, you know, entirely missed the tree.
        Sometimes a bull will close upon a man
and only catch his garments on its horns.   1110
A ship comes into port, wind at its back,
that lately lay along a hostile shore.
        Perhaps fire will consume a lofty seat
and spare the humble farmer in his croft,
and hail will leave a field of wheat alone.   1115
        The king, the tree, the man, ship, cottage,
                                              wheat,
live free of war, fire, horns, ocean, and hail,[22]
and I, too, safe and sound, pursue my hopes.

ACT III

[*Enter Antonio and Bernardo*]

(4) BERNARDO: Please go on with your story, Antonio,
for this is the strangest chain of events
that the world has seen in mortal memory.

ANTONIO: Fearing that worse harm might result,
she pretended, Bernardo, to dismiss me from the
house.
As a result, I spent two years in Naples.   6
From there, with the enemy off his guard,
I came to Ancona, and in secret once more
with heaven sole witness to my felicity,
travelled by night, and in short, dear friend,   10
with Livia opening a little door,
I enjoyed my lady's lovely person.
But now that we know for a certainty
she is pregnant a third time — ah, sweet heaven! —
it is settled that everything must be made public.
And in order to make all our vigilance sure,
she has feigned a vow to visit Loretto,   17
fleeing Ottavio and his jealous watch
and leaving her son, who has grown gallantly,
to take over governance of the estate.   20
It has turned out better than we had planned.

BERNARDO: Has she left her house and her vassals then?

ANTONIO: She could not endure my lengthy absence
and her fears for this third pregnancy.
From Loretto she proceeded with all good speed
under pretence of seeing this city of Ancona.   26
I hope today I shall have her before me.
And as love must redeem any fault of ours,
she intends to declare she is with her husband,
whom she values more than an emperor's crown.

	When all of Italy hears of it,	31
	as unequal a match as it is,	
	at least they will know it was proper marriage.	
BERNARDO:	Her brothers will be beside themselves.	
	They will come for you.	
ANTONIO:	No one doubts they will.	

When all of Italy hears of it,   31
as unequal a match as it is,
at least they will know it was proper marriage.

BERNARDO: Her brothers will be beside themselves.
They will come for you.

ANTONIO: No one doubts they will.
But I trust that for two such worthy princes   36
    the naked sword that is drawn against me
will be sheathed by pity for their niece and nephew;
nobility seconds blood in that.
    My two small angels arrived today   40
with a shepherd, dressed like a shepherd's children.
Eight years they've been exiles from their parents.

BERNARDO: Antonio, I fear those brothers of hers
very much.

ANTONIO: To be sure, they are powerful men.
But I think they will be human in this.   45

BERNARDO: May heaven reach out a clement hand
to take the vengeance from their hearts.

                                        [*Enter Lucindo*]

LUCINDO: Give me a guerdon for happy news.

ANTONIO: Has the Duchess come?

LUCINDO: The heavens, sir,
have granted your prayers. She's arrived in Ancona.

ANTONIO: No man living has more to be thankful for.   51
    A blessed life that redeems any death!
Let the lords of Aragon kill me then;
this crown will fulfill a humble man!
    Ah heaven, for just such lofty risk   55
a prince covets life.

BERNARDO: It is lofty indeed,
but the danger you place yourself in is great.

ANTONIO: Let me live with the Duchess a single hour
in the joy of being man and wife;
then whoever it grieves may strike me dead.   60
    Come, let us receive her; bring my children.
She will know if they are truly hers
if they, without winking, can look on her.[23]

BERNARDO: As misfortune has already looked, great lady.

                [*They exit; enter as many Servants as possible,
                and the Duchess and Livia, in travelling clothes;
                Urbino, the secretary; Celso, Furio, Dinarco, and Filelfo*]

(3) URBINO: But why do you mean, good madam,   65

	to put up at the house of Antonio?	
DUCHESS:	To show him by this means	
	that I pardon him, Urbino.	
URBINO:	But suddenly, six years after	
	he left your house in disgrace,	70
	having given you, not accounts,	
	but deceits for your estate,	
	you arrive at his house like this!	
	Are there no other seignories here?	
DUCHESS:	In my opinion the best ones	75
	are the ones whose lords you know.	
URBINO:	Antonio is poor, my lady.	
DUCHESS:	Is he lacking a bed and a table?	
URBINO:	There's no answering you today.	
DUCHESS:	This is my pleasure for now.	80

[*Antonio and Doristo enter with Alejandro,*
a boy in peasant's clothes, and Leonora,
a little girl, likewise in peasant dress]

ANTONIO:	Madam, does Your Excellency	
	mean to honour my poor house?	
DUCHESS:	Oh, Antonio!	
DINARCO:	What is happening here	
	is enough to try all patience!	
FURIO:	Be still. It is more than proper	85
	that we should stay in the house	
	of a servant so knightly and honest.	
ANTONIO:	Let me kiss your feet, my lady.	
DUCHESS:	Stay, Antonio. Things must be	
	conducted differently.	90
ANTONIO:	Lady, I wish to offer	
	two angels for your heavenly sphere.	
DUCHESS:	Who are these little shepherds?	
DORISTO:	They are my children, my lady.	
ANTONIO:	Give them your blessing, madam.	95
	My children, kiss her hand.	
ALEJANDRO:	What great love has come over me	
	from the moment I saw this lady!	
LEONORA:	I, too, Alejandro. I feel	
	my heart is moved inside me.	100
DUCHESS:	Have you a mother?	
ALEJANDRO:	She's dead,	
	the mother that took care of us.	
DORISTO:	Death is the end of all things,	

	but it took her unseasonably.	
DUCHESS:	And you, what is your name?	105
ALEJANDRO:	Alejandro, my ladyship.	
DUCHESS:	And you, my dear?	
LEONORA:	Leonora.	
DUCHESS:	Fear and love. What do you stay for?	
	Why have I come if not	
	to fulfill a just resolve?	110
	This is the moment at last:	
	they must learn why I have come.	
	Attend me now, my friends,	
	while I make my purpose known;	
	so that you may understand	115
	why I come here as I do.	
	The time for silence is over,	
	and if I was silent so long	
	it was only to await this day.	
URBINO:	Heaven help me! What's this?	120
DINARCO:	Madam, you cast your servants	
	into great confusion here,	
	with the intimation of this.	
	Speak; we all attend you.	
DUCHESS:	You know already, friends,	125
	that the death of the Duke my lord	
	left me still very young; my estate	
	had an heir but no government.	
	I sent, therefore, to Naples	
	for Signor Antonio, a man	130
	whose mind and person and worth	
	we and all Italy know.	
	But as the excellence	
	of his abundant merit	
	gave me occasion for it,	135
	I cast my eyes on him.	
	Let this not appear to you	
	any novel case in this world,	
	since you see in the *Triumphs* of Petrarch[24]	
	the example of how love conquers.	140
	I did not disgrace my honour	
	by seeking such remedies	
	as those who recount her deeds	
	have written of Semiramis.[25]	
	Before my lord Antonio	145

so much as laid a finger on me,
I was his wedded wife
and married to him in secret.
By him as my husband
Have I had these two children;   150
no children were born to Livia
as some jealous tongues suggest.
They have been raised in the mountains,
and the birth of the second one
obliged me to banish from my house   155
the man who was lord of it.
It is this exile, friends,
that has turned speculation loose:
my weeping eyes are weary,
my years are all undone,   160
my brothers hold me suspect,
my honour is full of suggestion.
And thus, to make an end,
I have come home today to his house.
Friends, Signor Antonio   165
is my husband, nor do I wish
for title, estate, or lands,
for revenues, vassals or kingdoms.
I leave my estate with a lord: 170
the young Duke is now a man
and can govern his own domain;
the Duke can gird on a sword
with which he can defend you,
provide you with succession   175
by means of marriage to an equal.
Any who wish to go
will have letters and money provided.
Any who wish to remain
will have a house and my love.   180

URBINO: So?
FURIO: I am beside myself.
URBINO: And you?
DINARCO: I am dumbfounded!
Let the eldest of us speak.
CELSO: I will speak as the eldest one.
Madam, on a thing so far done   185
that there is no human cure
which can serve to undo it again,

there is no use for advice.
This circumstance must provide
food for talk to Spain and Italy,   190
and subject for thought to your brothers,
and cause to your kin for some feeling.
God placate all of them,
for only God can do it.
And so He will because   195
this love is a licit marriage.
These white hairs and these arms that held you
when you were a year old, and less
— how can they leave you now
for any regard or fear?   200
This my short life, my lady,
I offer, to receive at your side
either pardon or the knife,
for I cherish no life without you.
I shall serve Signor Antonio   205
of whose merits I need not speak
since you chose him for your master.

DUCHESS: Do not weep, father, nay, for I   210
have put my faith in heaven
that my brothers may be moved
by the blood of theirs that's in me,
by the innocence of these children,
and by the mind and courage   215
of my lord Antonio, of whom I,
being who I am, am not worthy.
Why are you silent, Furio?

FURIO: For such reasons, madam,
that I have not dared to speak
lest I should speak what I feel.   220
Ah, madam, how many times
I have had misgivings of this.
How many signs your eyes,
the tongues of the heart, let slip!
And now there is nothing to say.   225
Pardon me if I take my leave
of your service from this day on,
preserving the respect that's due
to your son, Amalfi's Duke.
I return to his service, then,   230
for the Duke his father's sake

whom you have so greatly wronged.

[*Exit Furio*]

DINARCO: Lady, I have many things
to consider in this misfortune,
which oblige me to take my leave, 235
and not the least of them
is the danger that hangs over you.
God shelter and give you comfort;
but I am poor, as you know,
and I must provide for myself. 240

[*Exit Dinarco*]

FILELFO: If your estate's affairs
had a different Filelfo, madam,
one that could comprehend them
as you have arranged them now,
then he would stay with you. 245
You know I'm not able to.
Give me freedom and your hands.

DUCHESS: My friend, I am very grateful
that you return to the Duke.

FILELFO: I go back for the reasons I gave you. 250
May heaven shelter you.

[*Exit Filelfo*]

URBINO: Although I might be swayed
by these barbaric examples,
I condemn their examples instead.
I wish to serve Signor Antonio 255
as I have served yourself.
Who was worthy to be your husband
— why should he not be my lord?
Upon my knees I beg him
if out of love or jealousy 260
I have given him cause for grief
that he pardon me.

ANTONIO: Rise up.
Rise, Urbino. For myself
I considered you always, and still do,
as a brother and a friend. 265

DUCHESS: Urbino, I am indebted
to your love, and thus I swear
by the life that I hope my husband
may yet enjoy, to show you
how extremely grateful I am. 270

URBINO:	Madam, Your Excellency . . . .
DUCHESS:	I take leave of excellencies.
	Now Amalfi has its Duke,
	I shall be what Antonio is.
	I desire neither lands nor life.
	I am his. And very soon, Livia,
	I shall marry you to Urbino,
	for although I am poor and untended
	I have the means for your dowry.
LIVIA:	I kiss your feet and your hands,
	to serve you is payment enough.
	You may take my very blood
	if you should have need of it.
DUCHESS:	Doristo, you have borne yourself
	like a good and honest man.
	Change these garments; I wish you
	to accompany me.
DORISTO:	My lady,
	I am happy to hear that you do.
	They would have got rid of me,
	but I could not part with them,
	These two angels, my children,
	take me prisoner with their dear love.
	They could give me a thousand blows
	and I'd take it like a dog;
	I'd let myself be killed on your doorstep
	for fear of losing them.
DUCHESS:	And now it is fitting, Antonio,
	that we give them other garments.
ANTONIO:	It is fitting, since the world knows now,
	my sweet lady, that they are yours.
DUCHESS:	Well, let us go, and we'll join
	what I bring with what you have,
	since for two that love one another
	wealth is the least concern.
	We will set up our little house.
	And with you, my forever beloved,
	a gown of sacking cloth,
	a shirt of sailor's canvas,
	will be cloth of Milan to me,
	will be fine as Flemish cambric.
ANTONIO:	I answer you with tears
	for with words I can say nothing.

Line numbers in right margin: 275, 280, 285, 290, 295, 300, 305, 310

[They exit; Julio de Aragon
and Ottavio de Medici enter]

(4) JULIO: If my brother the Cardinal knew of it,
by heaven, Ottavio, I do believe
that the world in arms could not prevent   315
his running his sword through the villain's heart.

OTTAVIO: Julio, the deed is more licentious
than anything ever done by a noble woman.
With her servant, with Antonio?

JULIO: Ah,
madwoman, to be so young and so shameless.

OTTAVIO: Antonio de Bolonia is a gentleman,   321
but not the equal of such a great lady.

JULIO: Never doubt I resent this bitterly.
A commoner as my brother-in-law!
If I set any store by a lunatic passion,   325
for I'm sure she adores this infamous cur,
I would still have her do us the wrong in secret,
fulfill her lust like the thing it is.
       But to marry in so insane a way
that she leaves her house, her lands, her son —   330
this folly of passion cannot be excused.
Aragon blood has been outraged,
debased by so vile a brother-in-law.
But I will have vengeance by my own hand,   335
without the Cardinal my brother's knowledge.
       By the living heaven, it is our shame
that the Duke my nephew should have Antonio
as a father, a vile affront to heaven,
a raving madness to think such a thing!   340

OTTAVIO: Then, Julio de Aragon, my right hand,
I vow as the Medici I am, as a lover
who sees outrage and shame before his eyes,
to wreak the vengeance my mind conceives.
       As secure as they think to live in Ancona,
there are hirelings and pistols, and there are
                                                soldiers,
or I will kill him in my own person.   347

JULIO: For that, Ottavio, there are hirelings enough.
The more I think, the more I enflame
to be harsher still, that wretched siblings . . . .

OTTAVIO: They have given two fine ones to the Duke.   351

JULIO: They do not deserve to live infamously.

OTTAVIO: He has them secretly up in the hills,
                dressed in the habits of rustic peasants.

JULIO: Oh, these are gallant kin indeed   355
                to be brother and sister to so great a lord!
                Let us go, Ottavio, for I promise you
                I will take vengeance with my own hands.
                Ah, treacherous Duchess!

OTTAVIO: Alas, my Duchess!
                Antonio must die. I am sorry for thee!   360

                      [Julio and Ottavio exit;
             enter the Duke of Amalfi, son of the Duchess,
                  Furio, Dinarco and Filelfo]

(3) AMALFI: The Cardinal knows it already,
                all my kinsmen, my uncles, too.

FURIO: They take it very ill
                that a woman in her high position
                should commit such egregious folly.   365

AMALFI: How could my mother do it?
                How could she do something so mad,
                a dishonour to our blood
                that neither honour nor my love   370
                could restrain her from carrying out?
                  God help me! She loved this Antonio
                more than she loved me, her son!
                Oh mother, wretched woman!
                I wish to heaven I had died
                the day you gave birth to me!   375

FILELFO: Your Excellency, my lord,
                don't weary and wear yourself out
                with this ferocious sorrow.

AMALFI: Anyone who tells me that
                doesn't know how fierce honour is: 380
                  Eight years this infamy
                has been going on in secret.

DINARCO: It was murmured about by some;
                but they were afraid to speak outright,
                and finally silenced themselves.   385
                  There were certainly signs enough;
                Ottavio was always hinting,
                but no one believed him, my lord,
                because the manifest virtues
                that one could see in my mistress   390
                  were so much more powerful.

AMALFI: Feigned, they were all feigned.
              Have I a stepfather then?
              I'm Antonio's son?
FURIO: No, my lord.   395
              Your father is he that conceived you,
                  not he that cared for you.
AMALFI: Now that she's married him,
              and has been, in effect, a woman,
              and, like a woman, erred,
              there is nothing more to say.   400
                  Had she thought of me, been my mother,
              not demeaned me in this way,
              not left without seeing me . . . .
              But I am too old to require
              that all caresses be for me.   405
                  There. Antonio's children
              shall have her love, since for their sake
              she made this lowly marriage.
FILELFO: Are you not jealous, my lord?
AMALFI: Jealous? No, you insult me.   410
                  As God lives, I should take my brother
              and my sister into my soul
              if they were before me now!
              They are not such low-born creatures
              if you give it some proper thought.   415
                  Antonio, is he not a nobleman?
FURIO: Yes, my lord.
AMALFI: Well then, the portion
              that I give them from my mother
              will fill out what their father has,
              though he be but a poor gentleman.   420
                  Write — upon my life! —
              great honour and praise of Antonio
              to my uncles.
DINARCO: Blest be the day
              you were born!
AMALFI: And put down these calumnies
              with a fitting and proper boldness.   425
                  Say great good things of him.
              For my part, I think I shall do
              whatever I can to praise him.
FURIO: We give you a thousand thanks
              in her name, my lord, and in his.   430

AMALFI: Let no one speak ill of Antonio
in my house on pain of leaving it.
FURIO: Was there ever such a noble heart?
AMALFI: Well, it will be a good thing, friends,
to help her in such an hour.   435
              What did she take?
DINARCO: Just her plate,
jewels, bedding, and clothes.
AMALFI: No more?
DINARCO: Just that, no more.
AMALFI: This love is as nobly pursued
as the models of ancient times.   440
              Twenty-five thousand ducats
— get it if you have to borrow —
and take it off to them
to set up their house.
FURIO: You surpass
all examples in magnanimity.   445
AMALFI: Five thousand to my brother and sister;
take that much to them for clothing.
Let them throw off their peasant dress.
DINARCO: The Greeks, the Romans, the Persians,[26]
would be put to shame by you.   450
AMALFI: Come then, let's go write
to every last kinsman we have
in the house of Aragon,
and tell them there are sound reasons
we should honour Signor Antonio.   455
              Call him "Signor Antonio"
since he is her honest husband.
Ah, Duchess! Who will blame you
if womanhood pleads for you,
and then love, which is a devil?   460
              [They exit; enter the Duchess, Antonio,
                                and Urbino]
URBINO: You must both make haste to flee:
everything tells you that;
for I'm sure they are hot on their way
to redress their injury.
              Now see if I wasn't right   465
when I counselled you in Ancona.
DUCHESS: My own blood will not pardon you?

	No pity in my own kinsman?	
	And now my brothers pursue me.	
	What can they want from me?	470
ANTONIO:	My blood. I am what moves them.	
DUCHESS:	There are other reasons, Antonio,	
	that should move them to compassion.	
ANTONIO:	If we can get to Venice,	
	I'm sure if we once get there	475
	our lives will be safe and free.	
	I hope for great favour, my lady,	
	from the Republic of Venice.	
URBINO:	You must press on with even more fury;	
	the whole world comes after you.	480
DUCHESS:	I cannot press on, Urbino,	
	without my children.	
URBINO:	Here they are.	

[*Enter Livia and the children*]

	Ride on — alas, sweet heaven —	
LIVIA:	as if terror had feet of its own.	
	A man has just informed us	485
	that as he was leaving this spring	
	he saw soldiers in the forest,	
	an entire squadron assembled.	
	They can have no clear idea	
	of what you are planning to do;	490
	but if you move so slowly	
	some news is bound to reach them.	
DUCHESS:	Ah, children of my soul,	
	I tarry only for you.	
CELSO:	Flee, my lords, for God's sake!	495
	We have seen a spy about	
	that crossed our very path,	
	and when he saw us he fled.	
ANTONIO:	On horseback or on foot?	
CELSO:	On foot, and when he passed us	500
	he had an arquebus,[27]	
	and turned his head, looking about.	

[*Enter Doristo, now dressed as a squire*]

	Go, go quickly, my lords!	
DORISTO:	Death is imminent! Fly!	
	Mounted up on that ridge	505
	I saw soldiers marching on the plain;	

	they are coming in search of you.	
DUCHESS:	Flee, my beloved Antonio.	
	Flee, my darling; what harm	
	will my brother do to me?	510
	The tyrant is looking for you.	
	You are the object of his vengeance.	
DORISTO:	My lord, although only yesterday	
	I lived a rustic on a mountain,	
	you know that I know what is honour	515
	and what is cowardice.	
	It is no cowardice to flee	
	when the whole world comes after you.	
ANTONIO:	Don't you see, Doristo, that I fear	
	the loss of my wife more than death?	520
CELSO:	If you credit these white hairs,	
	they advise you to flee, my lord.	
	Take an old man's advice for once,	
	the more so when the case is so plain.	
	Urbino will remain here with them;	525
	and I shall remain here, too.	
DUCHESS:	Flee, my lord, my beloved;	
	flee if you feel for me.	
	Do not leave me without a husband	
	or your children fatherless.	530
ALEJANDRO:	My lord, my mother speaks wisely,	
	and I also beg you to flee.	
	Flee, so that you can come back;	
	don't let yourself be killed.	
LEONORA:	Father, why do you stay here?	535
ANTONIO:	I stay to defend you, sweetheart.	
LEONORA:	But you will have us killed.	
ANTONIO:	Children of my soul,	
	if this be not cowardice,	
	my blood apostate to yours,	540
	abide with God, and may He guard you.	
	Take these embraces then,	
	and keep these tears with you:	
	it is fitting a coward should weep.	
	And you, the sweetest treasure	545
	of my hopes and of my life,	
	you must pardon me this flight	
	since you command it, too.	
	Livia farewell, and Urbino;	

	my Doristo and Celso, farewell.	550
DUCHESS:	You carry my soul with you.	
ANTONIO:	I shall travel a wretched road.	

[*Exit Antonio*]

DUCHESS: Children, come stay by me,
for I shall have need of you.

LEONORA: Then you will not see him again?   555

DUCHESS: I don't know; I was born to weep.

ALEJANDRO: There, there, madam; I myself
will go to speak with my uncle,
the Cardinal.

DUCHESS: Don't say such a thing!
He's denied all kinship with us.   560

ALEJANDRO: By my faith, if I were grown
I would give Julio my challenge.

DUCHESS: Now heaven alone protects me.

LEONORA: Trust in heaven, madam.

DUCHESS: The Duke my son abandons me;   565
Julio de Aragon pursues me;
the Cardinal persecutes me;
my Antonio is wrested away.
          Then let death come for me now;
for that's the final remedy.   570

LEONORA: Mother, have faith in God,
that He will show His mercy.

[*Enter Julio de Aragon and Ottavio
with four Servants carrying arquebuses
and halberds*]

(4) OTTAVIO: There they are.

JULIO: Stand, cowards,
vile, obscene, forsworn, mad cowards;
stand and face my outraged fury.   575

DUCHESS: Who is here to oppose you, brother?

JULIO: Am I your brother? Do you say so, hussy?

DUCHESS: Are you Julio de Aragon?

JULIO: I am.

DUCHESS: Then am I not your sister?

JULIO: No, wench.
The Duchess of Amalfi, who is now dead,   580
she was my sister.

DUCHESS: And am I not she?

JULIO: Why, what a joke! Ottavio, listen.
The wife of Antonio de Bolonia tells me

that she is my sister, and what's more, feigns
to be Duchess of Amalfi.

OTTAVIO: Nay, my lord,   585
the Duchess of Amalfi would not have dreamed,
much less committed, so base an action.

DUCHESS: What, you here, too?

OTTAVIO: Who else but I?

DUCHESS: The Aragon blood is no business of yours.
Are you not a Medici?

OTTAVIO: Medici? Yes,   590
a line which boasts of pontiffs and kings.

DUCHESS: But how related to the Aragons?

OTTAVIO: By friendship, which is the most noble of kind
and is quartered in the arms of greatest honour.

DUCHESS: So your love ends here?

OTTAVIO: It has not ended,   595
nor shall it end while the cause still lives.

DUCHESS: Brother, oh, Julio, what do you want?

JULIO: Who are those children?

DUCHESS: Your nephew and niece.

JULIO: How nephew? I have only one,
the Duke of Amalfi, and he is the son   600
of a man who was our equal in blood.

DUCHESS: And these are the children of such a man
as has no equal in virtue or in mind,
and all Italy knows and bears witness to that.
And these children you see and you despise   605
if they be not your kin are still my children.
If they lack a father, then heaven must do;
for heaven shelters those that men cast away.

JULIO: And heaven chastises those that offend it.

DUCHESS: I married as heaven has willed we should do   610

JULIO: You offend heaven's will. In what is it served?

DUCHESS: The greater error would have been not to marry.

JULIO: Then our shame might have remained a secret.

DUCHESS: What shame to you if I am married?

OTTAVIO: Leave this. Why bicker with one who offends you?

DUCHESS: Jealousy never thinks well of love.   616

OTTAVIO: I am not jealous; I am wronged.

DUCHESS: Wronged? When was I yours? How wronged?

OTTAVIO: Is it not enough you deceived my hope?

DUCHESS: A mad presumption is not hope.   620

JULIO: So, enough. Where does your husband reside?

That fellow you call "Signor Antonio"?

DUCHESS: That Signor Antonio who is my husband
is in Milan.

JULIO: What, not with you?

DUCHESS: No, he knew your cruelty too well.   625

JULIO: No matter. Wherever he goes the Cardinal
will have friends, and I likewise.
Come, seize her.

DUCHESS: Seize me?

JULIO: Why, did you doubt it?

DUCHESS: How can you arrest me? For what crime?

JULIO: Is having debased and dishonoured my house
not crime enough?   631

DUCHESS: But by what order?
From the King? From the Pope?

JULIO: Mount up and ride.
And these, who are they?

URBINO: Her secretary.

JULIO: Why have you left the Duke?

URBINO: I have not
served the Duke, but only my lady.   635

JULIO: Who are you?

CELSO: One that raised her
and have borne her arms more than forty years.

JULIO: And you?

DORISTO: These children's foster father.
Yesterday shepherd for a hill and four sheep,
today a courtier to misfortune.   640

JULIO: Come Ottavio; the traitor was warned
and has taken off.

OTTAVIO: But tell me, Urbino,
Are you, too, accomplice to this crime?

URBINO: I do not see it is a crime to marry.

OTTAVIO: Is it not a crime that a woman disgrace   645
so many princes?

JULIO: Leave this now.
Anyone who wishes may go. I seize only
this woman here and her two children.

DUCHESS: What fault can these two innocents have?

ALEJANDRO: Will you arrest us too, my lord uncle?   650

JULIO: Uncle? I? What insolence!
Ride on to Amalfi.

DUCHESS: No matter now.

I know your intent is to keep me captive.
Kill me. But Signor Antonio lives.
                    [*They exit and Antonio enters*]
(3) ANTONIO: Where does my fortune lead me   655
with so shameful a flight as this,
abandoning my life
because I fear to die?
          Sad man, where am I going,
leaving my soul in the hands   660
of those two savage men,
to whom I give four lives:
          that of my beloved wife,
of Alejandro and Leonora,
children whom my soul adores,   665
and the one who is yet to be born?
          What man from such happy heights
has come to such depths as this?
Where shall my wretched heart
discover fortitude?   670
          How shall I find courage,
knowing that I have lost
four lives that I love so:
my children and my wife.
          Unless all the signs deceive me   675
all is already lost.
How the temptation comes
to fling myself from these rocks!
          O heaven, pinion my hands!
Pluck weapons away from me, heaven,   680
for amid such great affliction
human strength is of no avail.
          Alas, if they have perished
in the fury of his rage!
How is it I shun the rocks?   685
Have I not the right to be mad?
          Where am I to live,
sweet Camila, if I live without you?
Who has sundered us?
What man can divide you and me?   690
          Ah, my children, sweet warrants of life,
to be fated so cruelly!
                              [*Enter Doristo*]
DORISTO: I think these paths turn off

from the high road I was taking.
But in erring I've hit it by chance.   695
Signor Antonio!

ANTONIO: Doristo!
Is it possible I see you?
Am I as unlucky as that?
Have you fled? Have you abandoned   700
my children? Or are they dead?

DORISTO: Nay, rather they live more surely
than you ever in your life imagined.
They are on the way to Amalfi
— they must be there by now —
and everyone gives the fair Duchess   705
the heartiest congratulations.
The Duke her son came down
and rode out to receive her.
I saw them laugh at their ease
the greater part of the journey.   710
And the Duke embraced his brother
and his sister with great content,
and spoke earnestly with his mother
about this marriage of yours.
Whereupon Julio de Aragon,   715
the brother of the Duchess,
let it be known it pained him
you were absent on such an occasion.
For seeing the Duke is content,
they all press him to countenance you,   720
and have made him swear not to hold you
forever in disgrace.
This letter is from Urbino.

ANTONIO: Give me that and a thousand embraces,
for you are a thousand times worthy   725
of my arms and my heart, Doristo.
Then has it turned out so well?
Is it all disposed as you say?

DORISTO: I tell you just what has happened,
and also what I have seen.   730

ANTONIO: Heaven has been merciful!
I have more need of steadiness
to support this present joy
than I did for all my misfortunes.
[*He reads*]

"Events have turned out otherwise than we had expected: The Duke has been an angel of peace
against the fury of Julio de Aragon and Ottavio de
Medici. Do not keep yourself away, but look to what
may happen; for I trust in God that He will soon
make you easy.

— Urbino Castelvetro"

My soul and life's epistle,   740
I should kiss you a thousand times.
What reward can I ever give you
for returning my lost hope?
          Receive my happy tears
as your guerdon for good news.   745
Accept this much from a poor man
until he can make you a casket
          of gold adorned with pearls;
at such a time these words   750
must be cherished as they deserve
and laid into my soul.
          Is this true then, Doristo? Has the Duke,
my lord, done me this service?

DORISTO: He has tempered his uncle's fury 755
and his other kinsmen's, too.
          With an open heart he embraces
his mother, his brother, and his sister.

[*Enter Urbino*]

URBINO: It is vain to think I'll find him
by such uncertain paths!   760
          I shall lose both him and myself,
and I've left my horse for dead.

ANTONIO: People in this wilderness?

URBINO: What? I see people approaching.
God save me! Can it be?   765
Signor Antonio?

ANTONIO: Sweet heaven!
Is that Urbino?

DORISTO: I suspect
he has come for you if it is.

URBINO: Signor Antonio.

ANTONIO: Urbino!
What's this?

URBINO: I've come to fetch you. 770
And a thousand thanks to God

	for my having lost the way:
	in losing my way I have found you.
ANTONIO:	To fetch me?
URBINO:	Yes.
ANTONIO:	What for?
URBINO:	The Duke has smoothed it all.

775

He is the angel of this peace.
    He has done all like a prince.
Calm your heart, Antonio,
for Julio de Aragon
has let his wrath be calmed.   780
    And he writes this letter to you
because he has received some letters
that have obliged him to,
and continues to receive them,
    among them letters from the Cardinal   785
which command him not to touch you
on pain of incurring his wrath.
Because you are a man of importance
he would deal with you honourably.

ANTONIO: In the last, a Roman prince.   790

URBINO: Read and then ride.

ANTONIO: Is all well?

URBINO: All is well, by God!

[*He reads*]

"The Cardinal, my brother, has written me to leave
you in peace with your wife and children. Come for
them. Upon the condition that you go to Spain or
Germany to live, I am content to give them to you."

ANTONIO: How to Spain or Germany?
I will go to Constantinople.
For my children, I'll be like   800
a Hyrcanian tiger's dam.[28]
    Urbino, give me your arms.
Heaven takes pity on me.

URBINO: How well I deserve from you
these loving bonds, Antonio!   805
    Let us go now, my lord, for the Duchess
awaits you, and she gave me a thousand
messages.

ANTONIO: Ah, if only
I could fly, Urbino, I would!   810
    But we'll take horses. Come.

DORISTO: Let me serve as your guide, my lord.

URBINO: Ride, your lordship, ride,
           though we kill a thousand horses.

[They exit, and enter Ottavio,
Julio, and the Duke of Amalfi]

AMALFI: For the rest of my life, uncle,
           I shall be grateful to you   815
           for the goodness you have shown me.

JULIO: To serve you in this, nephew,
                   was only reasonable.
           If you are content with the case,
           then your contentment confers   820
           satisfaction on all concerned.

OTTAVIO: Now since we have supped together
           there is nothing more to do
           but to cast off our grievances
           and heal the incident.   825
               The Duke will succor his mother
           and they can go to Spain.

AMALFI: I wish that I could serve her
           with all my inheritance,
                   but aside from the estate   830
           entailed to the eldest son,
           I give her all the rest
           as if she only recovered
                   a lost security.
           And it grieves me to see her go.   835

JULIO: The Duchess must never return
           to Italy, nephew, ever.

AMALFI: She shall not if you do not wish it.

JULIO: Ottavio.

OTTAVIO: Yes, my lord?

JULIO: Why do you vex yourself?   840
               The Duchess has taken her payment,
           in the meal she has eaten just now,
           for being a vicious scourge
           on our offended blood.

OTTAVIO: What did you give her?

JULIO: I don't know.   845
           But she'll not survive half an hour.

OTTAVIO: Alas, unhappy lady!
           Unhappy stars attend thee!
                   Ah cruelty! O injustice!

JULIO: How can you say that, Ottavio,   850
           having seen so egregious a wrong?

OTTAVIO: I have not the heart for this.
           I loved her, adored her. I'll die!

JULIO: Hush! The pestilence take you!
           Don't let the Duke hear you.

OTTAVIO: Is it right   855
           that you have killed a lamb,
           an angel?

JULIO: Patience, Ottavio,
           or I shall forget myself!
           She is not an angel.
           A woman who wrongs her own blood   860
           and for such a flimsy caprice?

OTTAVIO: This was mad and cruel!

AMALFI: Ottavio, uncle, what's this?
           Is the anger not over with?

JULIO: He tells me that your mother   865
           could as well live here in Italy.

AMALFI: Well said. For my part, uncle,
           it would be a great consolation.
           If she might, I pray it of you.

JULIO: I say let it be as you will.   870

AMALFI: God preserve you a thousand years!
           [Enter Urbino, Antonio, and Doristo]

ANTONIO: I appear before them trembling.

URBINO: Here is Signor Antonio.

ANTONIO: I throw myself at your feet,
           and let my tears bear witness   875
           to my humility.
           I never truly believed —
           mad with so high a love —
           that I was as low as I am
           at the feet of Your Excellency.   880

AMALFI: Since my mother has given you to me,
           Antonio, as a father,
           I may call you father, then,
           once and a hundred times over.

ANTONIO: Father, my lord? Oh, no.   885
           I am not worthy of that.
           Your slave, yes. And as such
           I offer myself at your feet.

AMALFI: Rise, Antonio. You ought not

to be on your knees to me,   890
since God has sanctioned your house.
I am your junior, Antonio.
        Trust my good willingness:
I esteem you as a father;
for my mother gave me being,   895
and she gave you nobility.
        I love what she has loved;
I respect what she has respected.

ANTONIO: Your magnanimity
lets me hope all may be well.   900

AMALFI: Come kiss my uncle's hands,
His mercy is granted to all.

ANTONIO: Intercede for me, I pray you,
with such high Christian princes.
        Go before, great lord.   905

AMALFI: He is come, uncle.

JULIO: I know
who is come. I'll speak with him.

AMALFI: Be loving to him uncle.

ANTONIO: My lord, if Your Excellency
is offended, my humble life   910
is here to answer for it.

JULIO: [Aside]
Oh, God, with what patience I endure this!
[To Antonio]
        The Cardinal has commanded me,
Antonio, and I wish it as well,
that I should allow you your wife.   915
He does what needs be done.
        Go into those chambers
and prepare for your departure.

ANTONIO: My lord, this humble life
is delivered to your mercy!

JULIO: Get up, for your wife is desirous
of seeing you.

ANTONIO: I go,
my lord, to receive that favour
which you have accorded me.
        May heaven grant your life prosper,   925
and that of His Excellency![29]

AMALFI: Well done, and prudently.

ANTONIO: Jesu!

URBINO:	What a strange fall!
JULIO:	What was it?
OTTAVIO:	He fell as he entered.
ANTONIO:	Something is going to happen. 930
JULIO:	Something most gratifying.
	Here they are, waiting for you.

[Exit Antonio]

AMALFI:	Uncle, I promise you,
	I am infinitely gratful.
OTTAVIO:	Is it possible that I 935
	have aided in such madness?
	The pain will unseat my reason!
	But look, here Camila comes.
	Her face is calm and serene,
	and her colour is good. What now? 940
	Why, Julio must have deceived me
	knowing of my affection.

[Enter the Duchess and Livia]

DUCHESS:	Is the news certain then?
LIVIA:	Everyone says he is here.
DUCHESS:	I've come to see Antonio. 945
	They told me he had arrived.
AMALFI:	Haven't you seen him?
DUCHESS:	No.
LIVIA:	They must have been mistaken.
AMALFI:	Just now, madam, he went in.
	You simply took the wrong turn. 950

[Enter Fenicio, Julio's servant]

FENICIO:	It is all done, my lord.
JULIO:	You've not seen him?
DUCHESS:	No, I haven't.
AMALFI:	You came out to look for him
	while he went in to see you.
DUCHESS:	Well then, in that case, my lords, 955
	please send a page for him.
AMALFI:	Hola! Call my father.
JULIO:	How is it you give that name
	to the baseness of such a man,
	who has made your mother infamous? 960
AMALFI:	What, do we have this now?
	Isn't that finished with?
JULIO:	Finished? Yes, so much so,
	that we've called an end to this infamy.

Camila, if you wish to look upon   965
your children and your husband —
I say, on that insolent man
who presumed to call you his wife —
open the doors to that chamber
and deliver them up to her.   970
For we should give the Cardinal his way
and my nephew must be contented.
And prepare yourself to die.
Your trunk is already full up
with a most rapacious poison.   975
Ea, can't get them open?[30]

> [*Two doors are opened and a table is seen
> with three plates; in the middle the head of
> Antonio and on either side those of the children*]

DUCHESS: Whose could this cruelty be,
but that of an infamous monster,
who with smiling words and lies
has murdered him, my husband?   980
God will punish this!
My children, let all of us beg Him!
Clamour, you innocent babes!
Angels of the highest choir,
Plead for these earthly ones!   985
Justice, merciful Father!
Alejandro, Abel,[31] Leonora,
little girl, light of my eyes;
my husband and lord of my soul —
Antonio, beloved Antonio!   990

JULIO: The poison works; she falls!

OTTAVIO: Have I seen this, or are they fancies?
Ah heaven! But you have eyes.
Why do you not see this?
And why, if you have such ears   995
are you deaf to this misery?
Why do I care for life?

JULIO: What is this, Ottavio? Are you mad?

OTTAVIO: I am mad!

JULIO: Throw away your cloak?

OTTAVIO: My love's dead; throw it all away.   1000
For if the ship is drowned,
I fling all the treasure to the sea.
Camila, my Camila!

[Exit Ottavio raving]

AMALFI:	Why do you stare, savage tiger?	
	Why do you stare, Alban[32] lion?	1005
	Why do you stare, Spanish bull?	
	Draw your sword, you coward,	
	for from point to pommel I swear	
	I will dye this one in your blood.	
JULIO:	Nephew, you talk like a boy.	1010
	I have given you back your honour,	
	and this vengeance that I have taken	
	has been on your account.	

[Exit Julio]

AMALFI:	Vile and infamous, all of you!	
	I defy every one of you;	1015
	and I lay my hand on this cross[33]	
	not to quit it from my side,	
	not to dress in silk or gold,	
	not to eat from any raised table,	
	nor wear the Fleece on my shoulder[34]	1020
	till I have taken vengeance!	
	Look you, take up her body.	
URBINO:	Here the tragedy ends	
	which is entitled *The Steward*.	
	As it happened in Italy	1025
	you have seen it with your own eyes.	

NOTES

1 In Greek legend, Icarus was a youth who escaped from a tower by means of huge wings secured to his back by wax. Despite warnings, he flew too high and too near the sun. The wax melted, the wings dislodged, Icarus plummeted into the sea and was drowned.

2 Celso is poking fun at himself. Rodomonte is a swaggering braggart out of Ariosto's *Orlando Innamorato* and *Orlando Furioso*.

3 According to the Bible, the sin of the angel Lucifer, whose name means "light bearer," was ambitious pride. He led a revolt in heaven in order to

plant himself on the throne of God. The revolt was, of course, unsuccessful, and Lucifer and his followers were cast out of heaven into the pit of hell.

4 *Opportunity* or *Occasion* was often represented in the Renaissance as a female figure, with the tonsorial attributes described, standing on a globe. The expression "to seize Time by the forelock" recollects this. When Opportunity approached, one could seize her by the long lock of hair that grew near her forehead; but once she had passed, there was nothing to grab onto from the back.

5 These four lines accommodate an English-speaking audience. The original text merely explains that Urbino is joining the four letters into the words *oi no* (modern Spanish spelling: *hoy no*), meaning "not today."

6 The Real Academia Española text has a comma here, but it seems to me much more likely that this remark is addressed to the exiting Urbino.

7 The face of the sunflower turns slowly through the day, following the course of the sun.

8 See note 3.

9 In the Bible, Absalom was King David's beloved but treacherous son, who instigated an unsuccessful rebellion against his father. Absalom was killed when his long, golden locks became entangled in the branches of an oak tree in the forest. The mule he was riding bolted, and as he dangled helplessly by his hair he was riddled with darts by Joab and his archers.

10 See note 3 lines 485-87 and 853.

11 The audience is promised here that the actress who plays the Duchess may appear later on in breeches and form-revealing hose. Legal objections may have changed Lope's mind, however, since the Duchess is seen later only in the costume of a peasant woman and not in the clothes of a page.

12 When the play was written, of course (probably 1604-06), the century was still new.

13 A pun on the maidservant's name, which is pronounced [LEE' vyah]. In Spanish *Libia* and *alivia* are even closer in sound.

14 Zenobia was a third-century queen of Palmyra who greatly expanded the territories of the country while she ruled in the name of her son. To some her name represents unscrupulous ambition, but here she is clearly meant to be a paragon of chastity.

15 Crocodiles were said to sigh and moan and even to weep real tears while devouring their prey, in a bizarre charade of sympathy.

16 The chimera was a fantastic monster out of Greek mythology, but also any fleeting or fantastical image.

17 Either an amulet or a gesture with the hand, a good-luck sign.

18 The evidence at the end of the scene suggests that Urbino is not popular among the other servants. If he is perceptibly radiating smugness at this point, the reason for Furio's comment will be apparent to an audience.

19 Fabricio uses the word *dardos*, meaning "darts," or "harpoons," but I can find no record of harpoons actually designed to fly back in this dangerous way. It is remotely possible, however, that Fabricio is making garbled reference to an exotic weapon used to kill small game by the Tagalogs of the Philippines, which had been conquered and colonized by Spain in the middle of the sixteenth century. This compact weapon, fastened to the finger rather than the arm and designed to fly back into the hand on the force of the throw, is familiar to us now only as a toy. We still refer to it, however, by its Tagalog name — *yo-yo*.

20 Spain's most famous medieval epic *El Cantar de Mío Cid (The Song of My Cid)* tells us that the Cid kept a lion. The region of ancient Scythia stretched across what is now southern Russia, but Scythian power extended also into places in the Middle East which might well have grown lemon trees. Ethiopia, although close to the equator, boasts snow in its mountains. However, here all these things are supposed to be highly unlikely. Legend endowed chameleons with the ability to eat air and salamanders with the power to live in fire, but not the other way around.

21 Lope uses the Roman empress Faustina here, but Jezebel is more familiar to English-speakers as the paradigm of the immoral woman.

22 I have regularized the correspondence here slightly.

23 Here, as elsewhere, Lope compares the Duchess to the sun.

24 Francesco Petrarca (1304-1374) was a major Italian humanist and poet of the fourteenth century. The unfinished *Trionfi (Triumphs)* is a series of allegorical poems describing the triumphal processions of love, chastity, death, fame, time, and eternity.

25 Semiramis was a legendary queen of Assyria (probably based on the real Samuramat, ninth century, B.C.), and the subject, later in the seventeenth century, of an important play by Pedro Calderón de la Barca, *La hija del aire (The Daughter of the Air)*.

26 The Greeks, the Romans, and the Persians were all peoples reputed to have had the loftiest ideals of noble conduct.

27 The arquebus was a portable firearm developed in the fifteenth century.

28 From Hyrcania, a territory in northern Iran, part of the ancient Persian empire. For Lope a wild, heathen locale.

The protective maternal instinct has always been held to be particularly strong in savage animals.

29 *His Excellency* is the proper form for reference to a duke, and could refer to the young Duke of Amalfi. However, if Antonio is referring to the Cardinal, the correct form should be *His Eminence*.

30 Someone is either too slow or loath to open the doors.

31 This may be an appositive for Alejandro, as "little girl," and "light of my eyes" are for Leonora. It is also possible, however, that *Abel* is an epithet for the third murdered child (who is scrupulously counted elsewhere), the child in her womb. In either case, an allusion is made to the Biblical Abel, killed by his brother Cain; and the Duchess is accusing her eldest son of fratricide.

32 *Albano* can mean "from Alba Longa," but in this case it probably means "Albanian."

33 The sword held handle upward forms a cross, upon which knights traditionally swore their oaths.

34 One of the most illustrious orders of knighthood was the Burgundian Order of the Golden Fleece. The Young Duke removes the emblem which he wears around his neck: a broad gold chain with a pendant representing a loose ram's skin.